LIVING LIFE FORWARD

A Guide to Cutting Ties with the Bondages of Your Past

By
Rhonda Houston

Copyright © 2010 by Rhonda Houston

LIVING LIFE FORWARD
by Rhonda Houston

Printed in the United States of America

ISBN 9781609572716

All rights reserved solely by the author. The author guarantees all contents are original and do not infringe upon the legal rights of any other person or work. No part of this book may be reproduced in any form without the permission of the author. The views expressed in this book are not necessarily those of the publisher.

Unless otherwise indicated, Bible quotations are taken from New King James Version of the Bible. Copyright © 2010 by Xulon Press.

www.xulonpress.com

For Kathy;

To a long time, dear friend.

I pray God's richest blessings over you.

He is the Healer!

Jer. 30:17

Love,
Rhonda

Table of Contents

Introduction vii

Jesus, Our Liberator xiii

PART 1-THE CRISIS 21

   1. Bondage Exposed – Part 1 23

   2. Bondage Exposed – Part 2 35

   3. Bondage Perpetuated 56

PART 2-OVERCOMING THE CRISIS 73

   4. A Different Response to Bondage 75

   5. Taking the Time to Deal with Bondage 92

   6. The Signs of Bondage – Part 1 102

   7. The Signs of Bondage – Part 2 117

   8. The Signs of Bondage – Part 3 135

   9. Letting God be Our Fortress and Our Strength 145

PART 3-BEYOND THE CRISIS 157

   10. From Bondage to New Vision 159

11. Embracing Our Future 168
12. Choosing to See 181
13. Jehovah Rapha, The Lord Our Healer 197
14. Turning the Cursing of Our Past into the Blessing of Our Future..210

Conclusion 223

Introduction

Everybody has a past. Your past may consist of happy memories, good times, successes, and meaningful relationships or it may be full of struggles, dysfunction, disappointments, injustice, and bad memories. For most people it is a combination of all of these. No one seems to go through life without struggles in some area. However, wrestling with the problems of life is not always negative. In fact, we can actually allow those struggles to work to our advantage.

How is that possible? It becomes possible when we understand that *struggles can reveal hidden areas hindering forward movement in our lives*, areas making it difficult for God to bring about something new in His plan for us.

We could view it as getting "stuck" in certain places in our past. I grew up in Michigan. That means snow and snow very often means your car getting stuck as a result. I remember one particularly bad winter when I ended up in the ditch several times and needed someone to pull me out each time. That year it seemed no matter how diligently the salt crews worked, the roads stayed iced over. I thought those slippery roads were the reason for my little mishaps until one day I took my car in for some repairs and discovered I had a bubble on one of my tires. Amazingly, even though the roads remained icy, once the tire was fixed I stayed out of the ditches!

It seems life is somewhat like going through a Michigan winter. There will be difficult roads to travel and we may end up in a ditch from time to time. It's great when someone comes along and pulls us out, but it's even better when our life is in good working order and we stay out of the ditch in the first place! The good news is God has given us both instruction and promises from His Word to keep our lives in good working order so if we hit a slippery road we will stay on track with His plan and purpose for us.

God never planned for any of us to remain in a ditch living chained to our past but instead, for us to live our lives forward facing our future in Him. *It is a great day of freedom when we realize it is not so much our past holding on to us as it is us holding onto our past.* When we are willing to let go and follow God's command to move forward we will find that He has prepared a future filled with blessing and purpose for our lives.

I want to ask you an important question: *Are you in bondage to your past?* Bondage happens as a result of getting "stuck." One Bible lexicon defines the condition of *bondage* as "*slavery, servitude, and dependence.*" "*It is that state of man in which he is prevented from freely possessing and enjoying his life. It is a state opposed to liberty* (freedom)."[1]

Let me give you an example of bondage as it may relate to our past: Maybe a person grew up in a home where unrestrained anger was expressed. The lesson he or she learned from this environment is that anger is the way to respond to the pressures of life. Consequently, as an adult this person finds it difficult to control his or her anger when challenges arise. Uncontrolled anger is a form of bondage and it is definitely a problem that will hinder us in relationships, jobs, and in just about any other area we could name.

The more we become like Jesus, the more freedom from bondage we will experience.

When I have presented the *bondage question* to audiences in various places, I have seen many heads quickly nod as if to acknowledge, "That's an understatement!" At the same time, I have seen a look on other faces indicating they may have never thought along this line before.

Why would this be an important question to ponder? It is because getting "stuck" indicates we have gotten off track, we are spinning our wheels, and we have stopped making progress in our lives. For some it can mean an overall decline not only affecting them directly, but also everyone around them.

This is an issue not to be overlooked because the whole Christian life is about making progress.

Take a look at 2 Corinthians 3:18:

But we all, with unveiled face, beholding as in a mirror the glory of the Lord, are being transformed into the same image from glory to glory, just as by the spirit of the Lord.

Notice this verse states we are being changed from glory to glory. These stages of glory are each an increasing reflection of the glory of the Lord, *His character*, *His nature*, and *His actions*. Throughout our lifetime, God's plan is for us to continually make progress in becoming more and more like His Son Jesus. Each stage of this process brings us greater peace, greater blessing, greater stability, and more importantly, enables us to better reflect His glory to other people. The more we become like Jesus, the more freedom from bondage we will experience.

As we move forward in the pages of this book, a comparison will be made between two similar instances of bondage recorded in the Bible and how each was resolved. In the end we will discover that deliverance from bondage is *always* available to us through Jesus Christ; the One who has made provision to heal us in every area of our lives: *physically*, *emotionally*, and *spiritually*. To Him be the glory for His wondrous work in our behalf!

Jesus, Our Liberator

While I was ministering to a small group and finishing a lesson on how to biblically deal with worry and anxiety, a young man stood up and said, "I have had internal anxiety for as long as I can remember, and I have been convinced there was no way to be free from it. But after hearing what the Bible says tonight, for the first time I have hope that I can experience real peace in my life."

Struggling with worry and anxiety is one of the most common forms of bondage a person can experience, and just like this young man, we can easily be convinced it is a struggle that cannot be overcome. However, the Bible makes it clear that this bondage and others like it, is a battle that not only *can* be won, it *should* be won.

It is never too late to be set free.

As we pursue freedom from these struggles, there are two essential things we need to understand about bondage in our lives. First, we need to know that Jesus came to set the captive free; He is our Deliverer.

Consider Luke 13:10-17:

> *Now He was teaching in one of the synagogues on the Sabbath. And behold, there was a woman who had a spirit of infirmity eighteen years, and was bent over and could in no way raise herself up. But when Jesus saw her, He called her to Him and said to her, "Woman, you are loosed from your infirmity." And He laid His hands on her, and immediately she was made straight, and glorified God.*

The word *loosed* in this verse means "*to release as from bonds or imprisonment,*"[2] and that is exactly what bondage does. Whether it's physical, mental, or emotional, bondage can make you a prisoner. In John 8:32b Jesus gives us His response to bondage:

And you shall know the truth, and the truth shall make you free.

Here He is telling you and me that the truth in God's Word has, or *contains* the power to set us free.

Look at Galatians 5:1:

Stand fast therefore in the liberty by which Christ has made us free, and do not be entangled again with a yoke of bondage.

Freedom has been made available to us in Jesus and the truth of His Word, but we must make a decision to grab hold of it and refuse to let go.

The Process of Deliverance

Secondly, we need to know that deliverance from bondage is not necessarily instantaneous. In reality, it is better described as a process.

A good example of this is found in the book of Exodus, which focuses on the process of God loosing Israel from the bondage of Egypt. Exodus 2:23-25 records the culmination of this situation:

> *Now it happened in the process of time that the king of Egypt died. Then the children of Israel groaned because of the bondage, and they cried out; and their cry came up to God because of the bondage. So God heard their groaning, and God remembered His covenant with Abraham, with Isaac, and with Jacob. And God looked upon the children of Israel, and God acknowledged them.*

God heard the cry of Israel and instructed Moses to speak to them. Exodus 6:5-8 records His promise of deliverance:

> *And I have also heard the groaning of the children of Israel whom the Egyptians keep in bondage, and I have remembered My covenant. Therefore, say to the children of Israel: "I am the Lord, I will bring you out from under the burdens of the Egyptians, I will rescue you from their bondage, and I will redeem you with an outstretched arm and with great judgments. I will take you as My people, and I will be your God.*

> *Then you shall know that I am the Lord your God who brings you out from under the burdens of the Egyptians. And I will bring you into the land which I swore to give Abraham, Isaac, and Jacob; and I will give it to you as a heritage: I am the Lord."*

The word *rescue* in this verse means to *"to deliver, to be snatched out of, to save or to free."*[3] Notice, God said He would *rescue* (or deliver) them, and bring them into the land He had promised; however, they soon learned that this Promised Land contained enemies which had to be driven out. This seemed to the Israelites to be an overwhelming task except for the fact that God promised them He would be with them every step of the way to ensure their success (Exodus 23). In verses 29 and 30 He specifically described how this success would come:

> *I will not drive them out from before you in one year, lest the land become desolate and the beasts of the field become too numerous for you. Little by little I will drive them out from before you, until you have increased, and you inherit the land.*

Again in Deuteronomy 7:22-23, God caused them to see that their deliverance and victory would come by His might and power:

And the Lord your God will drive out those nations before you little by little; you will be unable to destroy them at once, lest the beasts of the field become too numerous for you. But the Lord your God will deliver them to you, and will inflict defeat upon them until they are destroyed.

To be sure, Israel had an immediate need for deliverance from the nation of Egypt, but once that deliverance came, there would be more battles ahead to be won before they could enjoy the fullness of what God had promised them. For them it would be a process, and in the end it is no different for us.

It is Never Too Late

So far we have seen that Jesus is our Liberator. The Old Testament saint looked forward to God's promise of Jesus and found freedom, we now look back on what Jesus has done in our behalf and we find freedom as well.

LIVING LIFE FORWARD

We have also discovered that deliverance is a process. However, there is one more area of instruction the book of Exodus gives us, and it is this: *It is never too late to be set free.* When their deliverance began, the Israelites had been in bondage, captive, and servants to an ungodly nation for approximately 400 years [17 years]. We also see in Luke 13 that the woman with a spirit of infirmity had been bound for 18 long years, yet Jesus said it was time to set her free.

In life it can be very easy for us to think something has gone on too long for there to be any hope of freedom. However, if we will look at the truth of God's Word, we will learn that this is never the case. Just like the woman who was bound, Jesus is saying to you and me, *"It is time to be set free!"* Amen!

PART ONE

The Crisis

CHAPTER ONE

Bondage Exposed – Part 1

When it comes to bondage from our past, one of the greatest hindrances to freedom is simply failing to recognize we have it. The very fact that it is tied to our past indicates it could be a condition we have lived with for a very long time. When this is the case, bondage can actually become accepted as the "norm" in one's life until it is exposed.

Based on my own life as well as the lives of those around me, I have come to the conclusion that crisis situations are one of the primary ways bondage in a person's life is exposed.

There is just something about the pressure of a crisis that can reveal the need for a change.

We live in an area that periodically experiences the effect of hurricanes. Not too long ago we went through one such episode. Upon returning to our neighborhood after evacuating, we saw an extensive amount of fence damage. We took note of one house in particular. Though we have a fairly strict covenant in our housing edition, its owners had always appeared on *the outside* to abide by it, yet their blown down fence surprisingly revealed they had broken nearly every regulation in the book including possession of a car on blocks!

This is a picture of the lives of many people. They are able to keep the appearance of a seemingly normal, well-kept life on the outside for all to see, but let a storm or a hurricane of circumstances come through and what has been hidden will be revealed.

There is just something about the pressure of a crisis that can reveal the need for a change, but I have also noticed there are times when we see bondage exposed in someone else's life that causes us to re-evaluate our own lives.

Whether it is a crisis in our own life or the revelation of bondage in someone else's life, one of the greatest places to observe how other people have dealt with these issues is in the Bible. In its pages not only are their challenges revealed, but also how they overcame and found freedom.

One such instance can be examined in the book of Exodus where we come upon a crisis involving the people of Israel. What makes this crisis even more revealing is the fact that we can compare it to a similar crisis found in the book of 2 Kings. As we follow through on this comparison, we will discover how one group of people chose to make a change while the other group chose to remain in their bondage.

We will also discover how their differing responses to the crisis at hand led them either in a direction of freedom and a future in God or a direction of continued bondage, never cutting ties to their past.

Bitter Waters can Expose a Bitter Heart

In Exodus 15:22-27 we begin to study about a challenge with bitter water that the people of Israel faced. Like many challenges we personally face today, this was one more situation that served to uncover the bondage they struggled with. As you read, notice the contrast between the response of the people and Moses' response to the same situation; *they complained while Moses cried out to God.* They saw problems while Moses looked for solutions.

So Moses brought Israel from the Red Sea; then they went out into the Wilderness of Shur. And they went three days in the wilderness and found no water. Now when they came to Marah, they could not drink the waters of Marah, for they were bitter. Therefore the name of it was called Marah. And the people complained against Moses, saying, "What shall we drink?" So he cried out to the Lord, and the Lord showed him a tree. When he cast it into the waters, the waters were made sweet. There He made a statute and an ordinance for them, and there He tested them, and said, "If you diligently heed the voice of the Lord your God and do what is right in His sight, give ear to His commandments and keep all His statutes, I will put none of these diseases on you which I have brought on the Egyptians. For I am the Lord who heals you." Then they came to Elim, where there were twelve wells of water and seventy palm trees; so they camped there by the waters. Exodus 15:22-27

At this point in scripture the Israelites had just experienced the miraculous Red Sea crossing under the leadership of Moses, as God directed them in their escape from

Pharaoh and his army. Great joy and rejoicing flowed from the people, so much so that in verses 20 and 21 Miriam, the sister of Moses, led all the women in dance and praise to the Lord for this great triumph.

Though spirits were high, it wasn't long before their song ended just as quickly as it had begun. On the other side of the Red Sea was the wilderness of Shur which had challenges of its own. Even before the people had time to fully catch their breath from the previous deliverance, they found themselves once again facing great peril. Three days journey had turned into three days without water. A feeling of desperation began to creep into their hearts. Had God forgotten about them? What if they could not find water for their children and livestock? What if they died right in the middle of the wilderness? Something had to happen, and quickly!

As they strained to see any sign of hope on the horizon, you can imagine their exuberance when they came to the waters of Marah. Surely this was their salvation; everything would now be okay, right? Wrong. They found the waters to be bitter and undrinkable. Within moments their exuberance turned to disbelief. "What is this, a cruel joke? How could this be happening to us? Once we left Egypt we thought things would be different. Moses, this is your fault!" And with that, the complaining and blaming began anew. Verse 24 tells us they complained about their circumstances and went on to blame Moses for them.

Moses recognized this crisis to be just another water challenge to be overcome like the Red Sea, and thus he cried out to the Lord for deliverance. Israel, on the other hand, saw it as one more injustice in their life to grumble about.

What was evident in Israel's response to their dilemma? Their dismay at meeting up with the bitter waters of Marah began to reveal the bitterness bound in their hearts. Instead of once again looking to God for help in their time of trouble, they allowed frustration to take hold of their emotions, and complaining and accusations to take hold of their tongues.

Do You Recognize the Waters of Marah?

Have you ever come across the "waters of Marah" in your life? Maybe you have come upon a situation and you thought, "This is it! This is what I have been waiting for! This is the answer to the emptiness or the loneliness or the discontent or the unhappiness; this is the answer to the thirsting on the inside of me."

Their dismay at meeting up with the bitter waters of Marah began to reveal the bitterness bound in their hearts.

Maybe it's a second marriage or a new job that hasn't turned out quite like you thought it would. It could be a distraction or something even more destructive like an addictive substance you thought would give you some kind of relief from the pressure you were feeling, and yet you find yourself more disillusioned than ever. Why? Because instead of quenching the thirst within, it seems you have only added to the pile of problems you were already dealing with.

Like Israel, there are people who have gone from one difficult *water* situation into another, and that is exactly what bondage tends to do in our lives; if we allow it to continue, it can lead us into one bad situation after another.

If this is you, there is reason for hope. Though they could not see it, the Israelites were actually in the right place at the right time and so are you. As we will see, God had a plan of deliverance for them and their situation, but somebody had to ask for it.

Meeting Up with Life

The fact is the situation in which the Israelites found themselves at Marah was not all that unusual. It is known today that brackish (salty) water was very common in that area at the time. Basically, these people had just met up with life. Despite their complaints, God was not trying to harm them in any way. On the contrary, He was showing them that He is the answer to any challenge living in this world might bring.

You and I can eliminate a great deal of bewilderment and confusion in our lives when we realize there will always be *Marahs* to deal with; places of bitterness in our relationships, our circumstances, and maybe even our health. Therefore, instead of being surprised by them, we need to understand that *our response* to these circumstances actually becomes a greater determining factor to our outcome than the circumstances themselves. Had Moses not responded as he did, Israel's response of complaining could have produced a completely different ending to the situation.

Just like Israel, how we respond to the pressures of life is crucial because it will indicate several things:

- *First, it indicates where our heart is.* Matthew 12:34b teaches us *"Out of the abundance of the heart the mouth speaks."* If we have bitterness, discontent, and complaining in our hearts, it will come out of our mouths. On the other hand, if we have peace and the joy of the Lord on the inside, it will also come out.

- *Secondly, it indicates where our focus is.* Hebrews 12:2a tells us we are to keep our eyes upon Jesus - not our circumstances – because He is *"the author and finisher of our faith."*

- *Thirdly, it indicates where our trust is.* Proverbs 3:5-6 says, *"Trust in the Lord with all your heart, and lean not on your own understanding; in all your ways acknowledge Him, and He shall direct your paths."* Are we to acknowledge our circumstances and frustration? No, we are to acknowledge our trust in God and His answer to our circumstances.

With the advantage of hindsight, we can see that Israel's response to the unfolding drama was tied to more than one event. At the same time they were complaining about the bitter waters, they were also displaying a complete disregard for the significance of the miracle they had witnessed at the Red Sea just three days before. An appropriate response to God's supernatural intervention on their behalf could have positively impacted how they now approached the challenge at Marah.

SUMMARY: *Bitterness Outside Can Reveal Bitterness Inside*

Many times, bondage from our past can be revealed in time of crisis. The bitter waters at Marah painted an accurate picture of the bitter bondage still locked in the hearts of the people. The key to healing this bitterness would come from understanding the importance of proper response to their circumstances.

Further Thought

1. Later in Israel's history, Judges 6 tells us they were experiencing oppression from enemy nations. This crisis exposed great fear in their lives. Instead of trusting in the God who had delivered them in the past, they chose to cower before their oppressors by hiding in dens and caves. As a result they were greatly impoverished.

Finally, the stress became so intense they cried out to God and He answered by reminding them He was the God who had brought them up from Egypt and out of the house of bondage. He had also previously told them they were not to fear these enemy nations because He had proven He was able to deliver them from oppression.

What enemies are you facing today?

> *Past Stronghold*

2. How are you responding to these pressures and what do you feel they have exposed in your life?

> *Weakness*

3. Are you struggling with fear because of your circumstances? Are you tempted to hide from them rather than trusting in the God who has delivered you in the past?

> *Fear of Letting Go*

4. What is God reminding you of today? Write down at least two instances where God has delivered you from oppression in the past.

CHAPTER TWO

Bondage Exposed – Part 2

The crisis at Marah teaches us that bondage in our lives will likely be exposed as we respond not only to negative circumstances, but also to positive circumstances we face. Do we struggle when difficulties arise and hardly even notice the answers to prayer God has brought our way? If so, it is time to consider how miracles can affect our present day Marahs.

There are many people today who would like to tell us that miracles have passed away and God no longer does such things, but that is not the God of the Bible.

Psalm 77:14 (NIV) says this of God:

You are the God who performs miracles; you display your power among the peoples.

We see miracles in the ministry of Jesus, miracles in the book of Acts, miracles in the ministry of Paul as well as others in the New Testament. So what exactly do miracles teach us and how can they affect our present day "Marahs"?

Just like the Red Sea, there are times in our lives when we will see God do miraculous things, and these miraculous events should serve as a guide for our future. First, they can anchor us to the will of God when the winds of circumstance begin to blow.

When my husband and I first moved to Houston, I pursued a job in the medical field. Even though I am a certified x-ray technician, I had not worked in this area of expertise for many years; therefore, it was very apparent God had worked a miracle to open a door of employment for me at a local clinic. To my husband Chuck and me, it was like God had split the Red Sea all over again. We were amazed at this answer to prayer; however, it wasn't long before I marched into the "Wilderness of Shur"! For one very long year, what kept me going in the midst of adversity was the encouragement I received from knowing God had placed me at that particular clinic. In the end, after many challenges and significant growth in my faith to handle them, not only did I increase spiritually but many doors to minister the gospel were opened to me. Miracles can keep us on track with the will of God.

Had Israel used the Red Sea miracle to anchor themselves to the will of God, their experience at Marah could have produced a great deal more than quenching the natural thirst in their lives. Marah provided them with an opportunity to learn how to better hear from God, how to follow His commands, and how to look to Him as their source of supply for everything in life.

Miracles also guide our future by changing our focus from our current circumstances to the true nature of God. Israel needed to understand one important aspect of the nature of God: *He does not change.* Hebrews 13:8 boldly declares:

Jesus Christ is the same yesterday, today, and forever.

When faced with a new challenge, we can and should understand that if God helped us and did miracles for us yesterday, He will certainly help us with our present difficulty. The fact that God has done miracles in the past ensures us He will do miracles again, not only today but also in the future.

In 1 Samuel 17:37a David made such a declaration in the face of Goliath's threat to Israel:

Moreover David said, "The Lord, who delivered me from the paw of the lion and from the paw of the bear, He will deliver me from the hand of this Philistine."

Even as a teenager, David knew how to draw strength from God's miraculous interventions in his past; if God delivered him in the past, He would most certainly deliver him again in present and future challenges.

The fact that God has done miracles in the past ensures us that He will do miracles again today and in the future.

In my own life, I have learned some important lessons about drawing confidence from God's goodness. At the age of 70 years old, my father suffered a heart attack and went through open heart surgery. As we stood in faith, my family and I witnessed God perform miracles in my Dad's physical body. Yet, even though he came through the surgery successfully and even though I clearly witnessed the delivering power of God in his situation, for approximately three months following his surgery I battled fear and anxiety over my Dad's health. Every little symptom he developed caused the fear in me to escalate. (I will talk more about my struggle with fear in Chapter Seven.)

Before leaving the hospital, we were given all types of pamphlets and information on what we might expect in my Dad's recovery. The pamphlets explained that this type of anxiety reaction was normal in supporting families and would usually continue for about six months. However, I knew biblically that God did not want me to live with anxiety and fear, so I continued to seek Him concerning my struggle against them.

One weekend I received a call from my parents informing me my Dad had developed a certain set of symptoms. Once again anxiety arose on the inside of me. Since it was the weekend, there was a waiting period to connect with the correct doctors who were on call. That night I went to bed fervently praying about the situation. I was awakened the next morning with Hebrews 13:8 ringing in my ears and the reality of that verse set me free once and for all. I finally had a revelation that if I could trust God to bring my Dad through open heart surgery, I could also trust Him with any other circumstances that might follow. Faith immediately replaced fear in my heart and I was free. Not only was I set free, but because faith was now free to flow in me, another answer to prayer manifested: *the symptoms in my Dad's body proved to be nothing serious.* God had been true to His word!

The Message of Miracles

To put it in simple terms, *miracles send a message that God is able and willing to help us in the difficulties of life.*

God's willingness to help is expressed in Psalm 107:31(NIV):

Let them give thanks to the Lord for his unfailing love and his wonderful deeds for men.

Notice, God's *"unfailing love"* is connected to the miracles He has performed. Through miracles God's willingness to deliver us is shown as His faithful love displayed in our lives. The *Theological Wordbook of the Old Testament* says it this way: *"It is of interest to note that the function of God's wonders is ultimately to make mercy available to the recipient."*[4]

Most importantly, miracles send a message to you and me that God is able to help us with whatever life sends our way. In Genesis 18 Sarah laughed at the thought of God's promise to give her a son in her old age, but God's response was, *"Is anything too hard* (wonderful) *for the Lord?"* Not long after, Sarah gave birth to the promised child and gained firsthand knowledge that *God is able.*

> ***Miracles send a message that God is able and willing to help us in the difficulties of life.***

When God did miracles through Moses in Egypt and at the Red Sea, He was sending a message to Pharaoh that He was the only true God and He was all-powerful. The same miracles also confirmed to Israel that God was able to deliver them, bring them out, and continue to provide for them.

When God shut the mouths of lions on Daniel's behalf, He demonstrated His ability to protect. When He brought victory to Gideon and his army of three hundred men, He demonstrated His ability to deliver us from enemies greater than ourselves. When Jesus fed five thousand people, He demonstrated His ability to provide the necessities of life. And when He healed the multitude, He demonstrated the fact that He is our Healer and no respecter of persons.

God desires to pour His love and mercy out upon us. He longs for us to recognize Him as the God of the impossible. Through miracles we come to the realization that God is able and willing to meet our needs.

The Proper Response to Miracles

How should Israel have responded to the Red Sea miracle? The Bible talks about three appropriate responses and all three will help us have the correct response when facing the Marahs in our lives:

1. **Remembrance**
2. **Thanksgiving**
3. **Belief**

Remembrance

Psalm 77:11-12 talks about the importance of remembrance:

I will remember the works of the Lord; surely I will remember Your wonders of old. I will also meditate on all Your work, and talk of Your deeds.

How do we remember God's miracles? By meditating on those miracles and talking to others about them. If we are meditating on and talking about all the wonders God has performed, we cannot be meditating on and talking about the negative circumstances we face.

Through the years we have experienced many miracles in my family, miracles we have not forgotten. Not only do we frequently reminisce and keep record of them, we also remind ourselves of them when we pray.

My mother, Joan, was the recipient of one of these miracles many years ago. When she was a young woman expecting her third child, she was told she had a hernia that would need to be repaired as soon as she gave birth. In the meantime, my mother was given a bulky brace to wear as a support. One night she attended a special meeting at her church. During the meeting she was prayed for by a visiting minister and was instantly healed!

A week later my mother began to experience discomfort where she had been healed. Being a new Christian, fear rose up that she had "lost" her healing, so she called one of the older ladies in the church known as Grandma Johnson. Not being one to mince words, Grandma Johnson came straight to the point: "Joan, either you are healed or you are not. Make up your mind!"

Right then and there my mother had a choice to make, become offended or accept the rebuke she had been given. She chose the latter and refused to let go of the healing she had received. Not long after, her doctor confirmed her healing but also commented that the proof of her healing would be if she ever had another baby. Approximately six years later she gave birth to my youngest brother providing testimony to the fact that she was truly healed. My parents still have the brace today as a reminder of God's miracle-working power.

Though it happened many years ago, my family still looks back to this healing as a memorial that God will continue to heal and deliver us today.

Thanksgiving

Along with remembrance, thanksgiving should also be a normal Christian response to miracles. Psalm 107:21-22 exhorts us to give thanks for God's wonderful works:

Oh, that men would give thanks to the Lord for His goodness, and for His wonderful works to the children of men! Let them sacrifice the sacrifices of thanksgiving, and declare His works with rejoicing.

In this Psalm the people are instructed to give thanks for God's wonderful works not only in their private time with God, but also in public. Luke 17:11-19 records the story of Jesus healing ten men of leprosy, yet only one man returning to give glory to God with a loud voice. Jesus questioned the one as to why the other nine had not also come and let the worshipping man know his expression of faith had made him whole. *Because this man had given thanks for one miracle, he experienced another in his life; he was now not only healed, but also whole.*

Thanksgiving should also be a normal Christian response to miracles.

Belief

The third response we should have to a miracle is belief. In John 2:23, many people believed on Jesus because of the signs He did and in John 5:36b Jesus gave explanation for this:

For the works which the Father has given Me to finish – the very works that I do – bear witness of Me, that the Father has sent Me.

Miracles should capture our attention and cause us to acknowledge that God is the Most High and there is no other to be compared to Him. Rahab came to a place of belief when she heard about the miracle at the Red Sea. In Joshua 2:10-11 she explained this realization to the two Israelite spies who had been sent to survey Jericho:

For we have heard how the Lord dried up the water of the Red Sea for you when you came out of Egypt, and what you did to the two kings of the Amorites who were on the other side of the Jordan, Sihon and Og, whom you utterly destroyed. And as soon as we heard these things, our hearts melted; neither did there remain any more courage in anyone because of you, for the Lord your God, He is God in heaven above and on earth beneath.

In 1 Samuel 17, David was confident that God was about to do a miracle by delivering Goliath into his hand. In verse 46 he declared what the end result of this miracle would be:

This day the Lord will deliver you into my hand, and I will strike you and take your head from you. And this day I will give the carcasses of the camp of the Philistines to the birds of the air and the wild beasts of the earth, that all the earth may know that there is a God in Israel.

Through miracles we come to understand the greatness of our God. When we remember them, talk about them, and give thanks for them they become an important indicator of what God will yet do in our lives.

What Miracles?

Miracles can anchor us to the will of God and focus us on the true nature of God, but what if you cannot identify any miracles in your life to remember? Amazingly, Israel complained of this multiple times throughout their journey, but nothing could have been farther from the truth for them. God had surrounded them in miracles.

Israel was surrounded by miracles; however, they couldn't see them because of the state of their heart.

Psalm 78 recounts the miracle of manna and fowl for the nourishment of the Israelites in the wilderness. In verses 23-28 we find that God opened the very doors of heaven to bring this wonder about:

Yet He had commanded the clouds above, and opened the doors of heaven, had rained down manna on them to eat, and given them of the bread of heaven. Men ate angels' food; He sent them food to the full. He caused an east wind to blow in the heavens; and by His power He brought in the south wind. He also rained meat on them like the dust, feathered fowl like the sand of the seas; and He let them fall in the midst of their camp, all around their dwellings.

If the Red Sea crossing had not been miraculous enough, now we have food being supplied from heaven itself. You would think any recipient of these awesome wonders would have been overflowing with great expectation for their future, but verses 32 and 33 paint a different picture:

*In spite of this they still sinned, and did not **believe** His wondrous works. Therefore their days He consumed in futility, and their years in fear.*

The key word in verse 32 is *believe*. In looking at this word *believe*, the *Theological Wordbook of the Old Testament* gives us the following insight:

*At the heart of the meaning of the root (believe) is the idea of **certainty**. And this is borne out by the NT definition of faith found in Hebrews 11:1. The basic root idea is firmness or certainty.*[5]

The New Testament definition for faith is found in Hebrews 11:1 (Amp):

> *Now faith is the assurance (the confirmation, the title deed) of the things (we) hope for, being the proof of things (we) do not see and the conviction of their reality (faith perceiving as real fact what is not revealed to the senses).*

The Berkeley Version of the New Testament translates the first part of Hebrews 11:1 this way:

> *But faith forms a **solid ground** for what is hoped for.* [6]

If we will embrace them, miracles can provide a firm foundation in our heart to release our faith for God's goodness to be experienced in our future.

As previously stated, God's wonders in our life can and should ignite belief on the inside of us. My husband, Chuck, tells the story of a time when he was at a low point and struggling with discouragement. It was very difficult to perceive God working in his life at all, let alone to believe there were miracles working on his behalf that could strengthen his faith. That is, until one morning he was driving to work and beheld the most beautiful sunrise he thought he had ever seen. In that moment he had a revelation: If the God I serve could create this miracle of beauty, then I know He is big enough to help me as well.

If we are willing to see them, where else can we find miracles to encourage our faith? Let me suggest several possibilities:

- *In the Word of God.* Old Testament and New we find testimonies of people having their needs supernaturally supplied. There we can read about people who were miraculously healed, people who were delivered from danger, and people who were provided for in time of lack or famine, and still others who were enabled to rise out of the ashes of overwhelming failure, going on to do great things for God.

- *In the testimonies of people around you.* There have been many times in the past I have been greatly inspired to believe God for my own deliverance because of the testimony of someone else around me. This encouragement comes from understanding that if God will do it for them; He will most certainly do it for me.

- *In the testimony of Jesus.* Romans 8:11 says, *"But if the Spirit of Him who raised Jesus from the dead dwells in you, He who raised Christ from the dead will also give life to your mortal bodies through His Spirit who dwells in you."* We have to understand that the Holy Spirit who brought about the miracle of the resurrection of Jesus Christ, is the same Holy Spirit who now lives in us as born again believers.

Israel was surrounded by miracles they couldn't see because of the state of their heart. And what was the state of their heart? Their constant complaining revealed it was full of bitterness and unbelief.

You and I also are surrounded by miracles from God, miracles from heaven itself. If you are unable to recognize them, it is time to consider the state of your heart.

In the next chapter we will further examine this symptom of unbelief called *complaining*.

SUMMARY: *Responding to Miracles as Well as to Difficulties*

Just like our responses to difficulties, our responses to miracles can have great impact on the outcome of the circumstances we face; they can also lay a foundation for miracles in our future. When we understand the purpose of miracles we are better able to have the proper response to them.

Further Thought

1. Have you ever considered that God could do a miracle in stages? In Mark 8:22-26 a blind man came to Jesus for healing. The first time Jesus laid hands on him the man's eyes opened, but not all the way, for he saw *"men like trees, walking."* The second time Jesus laid hands on him his sight was completely restored and he saw everyone clearly.

Zechariah 4:10 says that we are not to despise the day of small things. If God has begun a miracle in your situation, by all means, let Him finish it even if it is in stages. Do not let what still needs to be done overshadow what has already been done. Instead let the latter be a basis of faith for the former.

Has God done a "stage one" miracle in your circumstance? If so, can you continue to cooperate with Him and trust Him to finish what He has started?

2. In our "Further Thought" section of Chapter One, we looked at the plight of Israel in Judges, Chapter 6. In verse 13 the scene of the chapter now shifts from a nation in fear to an individual struggling with fear. When confronted by the Angel of the Lord, Gideon asks, *"If the Lord is with us... where are all His miracles which our fathers told us about?"*

God in His mercy and grace went on to give Gideon several miracles of confirmation. These miracles provided Gideon the courage to obey as God, one step at a time, went on to use him as a deliverer for his people.

Are you looking for God's miracles in your everyday life? If not, ask God to open your eyes to see the miracles of confirmation He is doing in an effort to build your courage to obey Him.

3. I encourage you to write down at least three miracles God has either done in your life or you have witnessed in someone else's life around you. Next, evaluate your response to these miracles. Do you need to see them in a new light today?

How can they strengthen you as you believe God to overcome in your present circumstances?

① Miracle of Zac's healing @ birth

② Miracle of the healing & restoration in Zac's marriage

③ Renee's ovarian cysts healed

④ Renee's glucose test coming back perfect

⑤ My back healed after PT was over

⑥

CHAPTER THREE

Bondage Perpetuated

And the people complained against Moses, saying, "What shall we drink?" Exodus 15:24

As we have already seen, complaining can be a symptom of unbelief in the heart, but it can also perpetuate the condition of bondage in a person's life. When we stay fixated on the negative, it can provide fertile ground for bondage to continue and even worsen.

For example: A person who has come out of a bad marriage could be in the middle of a second marriage and struggling. Instead of remembering and being thankful for what God has done in bringing this new person into his or her life, they fight fear that the new spouse will behave as the ex-spouse did. Even though the fear may be totally unfounded, it begins to manifest in faultfinding and complaining rather than believing that the God who brought them together is the same God who can keep them together.

In the case of the Israelites, instead of remembering, giving thanks, and rising up in belief in response to the miracles they had witnessed, they gave in to their emotions and fears and began to grumble and gripe. How many times have we done the same thing? Personally, I would say, more times than I would like to admit.

The Bible has much to say about this issue called "complaining" and none of it is good. Philippians 2:14, admonishes us to *"Do all things without complaining and disputing."*

Complaining is a first cousin to "worry and anxiety." You might even say it is the outward expression of worry and anxiety. When we yield to worry and allow anxiety to take hold, we find ourselves spinning our wheels and going nowhere toward a solution to our problems. Just like worry, complaining is completely unproductive; however, it is also an open door to some other areas:

1. Psalm 77:3b – *"...I complained, and my spirit was overwhelmed."*

The word *overwhelmed* in this verse means "*to faint or to be weak*" in the sense of mental or emotional exhaustion.[7] The reality of complaining is it can actually deplete the very strength we need to achieve a good outcome in our circumstance.

2. Psalm 106:24-25 – *"Then they despised the pleasant land; they did not believe His word, but complained in their tents, and did not heed the voice of the Lord."*

As we have already mentioned, complaining can also be a sign of unbelief and disobedience to God. First John 2:20 says, *"But you have an anointing from the Holy One, and you know all things."* In context, this verse is actually talking about having the ability to discern between true and false teachers of the Word of God; however, I believe there is something more we can understand.

The reality of complaining is it can actually deplete the very strength we need to achieve a good outcome in our circumstance.

A born again believer who has the Holy Spirit living on the inside of them is never in a place where he or she just does not know what to do. The Bible says we *"know all things"*. Right now you may be thinking, "But you don't understand. I am facing difficult circumstances and I really *'don't'* know what to do." In reality, you may not know every step needed to lead you out of your difficulty, but I guarantee you know the next step. We *always* know the next step. The next step is whatever the Holy Spirit on the inside has been prompting us to do; in fact, if we would think about it and be honest, we would find that He may have even been prompting us to do that very thing before the problem ever presented itself!

The issue is not whether or not we know what to do, but whether we will obey what we already know to do. Too many times it is easier to sit down and complain rather than obey God's prompting to spend more time in prayer or in His Word *or* His prompting to be faithful to be in church *or* to walk in love toward someone *or* to cast our care and put our trust in Him. The temptation to complain can become great when God calls us to trust Him a step at a time. Just like these Israelites, complaining on our lips is an outward sign that we have made a decision not to believe God's Word or to obey the prompting of His voice.

As they stood facing the bitter waters of Marah, did Israel know what to do? They most certainly did. Israel's "next step" was to trust God and follow the direction of the man Moses who God had placed in leadership over them; however, the people had also received instruction before they ever left Egypt.

Time to Complain or Time to Worship?

As we further examine this issue of "complaining," I believe there is a very important element in our text that must be considered. In his study on the significance of numbers in the Bible, E.W. Bullinger states that *three* is a number indicating completion. He makes the following observation regarding Israel's journey after the Red Sea crossing:

The complete separation of Israel is shown in "the three days' journey into the wilderness" (Exodus 5:3), marking the complete separation with which God would separate His people from Egypt then, and from the world now. We can understand Pharaoh's objection in first wishing them to hold their feast "in the land" (Exodus 8:25), and when that could not be, at last consenting to their going, but adding, "only ye shall not go very far away." So Satan now, is well content that we should worship "in the land"; and if we must go into the wilderness, that we should be within easy reach of the world and its influences. Not so Jehovah. He will have no such borderland service; He will have a "scientific frontier," a divinely perfect "three days' journey into the wilderness," completely separating them from all their old associations. The difficulty of "drawing the line," which so many Christians experience, arises from the fact that it is a crooked line, and that it is an attempt to include that which cannot be included. Drawn at a proper distance it can be ruled straight, and be divinely perfect and effectual. [8]

God was leading Israel into a situation where they could once and for all cut ties with their past. Bullinger points out, however, that Pharaoh was pressuring them to stay as close to Egypt as possible, thereby keeping ties intact and ensuring his continued control.

We see in this a picture for our lives. God wants to completely heal us and set us free from the control of our past, but Satan is pressuring us to not cut ties. One way he accomplishes his intention is by tempting us to complain.

Israel looked at the "three days journey," and the rest of their time in the wilderness as a time to focus on everything they felt God was *not* doing for them. This focus consumed their thoughts and they quickly turned to complaining.

> **God has given each one of us the gift of time, and what we do with that gift is a crucial decision for our lives.**

God, on the other hand, viewed this time from a completely different perspective. Before they ever left Egypt, God declared how they should spend their time in the wilderness.

In Exodus 7:16 the Lord directed Moses in the following way:

> *And you shall say to him (Pharaoh), 'The Lord God of the Hebrews has sent me to you, saying, "Let my People go, that they may serve Me in the wilderness." but indeed until now you would not hear!*

The word *serve* in this verse also means *"to worship"*[9]. Israel's "three days journey" and their remaining time in the wilderness were to be spent in service and worship before God. Actually, you could view this journey as a gift from God because it would afford them time for these pursuits that had not been available to them in Egypt.

Exodus 2:23 describes their experience in Egypt:

Now it happened in the process of time that the king of Egypt died. Then the children of Israel groaned because of the bondage, and they cried out; and their cry came up to God because of their bondage.

Part of the bondage they experienced in Egypt was the fact that Pharaoh had worked them to the point of exhaustion. There was no time left over for the service and the worship of God.

The Bible goes on to say God heard their cry and began leading them in the direction of deliverance. Now they found themselves in a place where the outward bondage of Egypt was gone, and time was made available to them for the worship of God. The question was *what would they do with this gift of time?*

As we look back over Israel's time in the wilderness, we clearly see God had already prepared answers for every need they would have. He had done His part, but the people made it hard on themselves by not doing their part, which was to worship rather than to complain.

God has given each one of us the gift of time, and what we do with that gift is a crucial decision for our lives. Again, did Israel know what to do with their time? Yes, and I guarantee, so do we.

Complaining caused Israel to be continually tied to Egypt.

I was recently talking to an elderly Christian lady who found herself frequently bored and depressed. When I mentioned this gift of time she had been given and how it could be wisely used for prayer, she replied by saying, "I guess that's all I am good for now."

How many of us have viewed the use of our time for spiritual things as a "bottom of the list" option? Or how many times have we thought, "I am just too busy for that"?

Whether you have been given a large amount of time from God or a small amount because of the demands of job and family, we must be wise stewards of this time. If we will be faithful to wisely use the time we have, we can trust God to give us more.

Have you ever noticed that right in the middle of our business, we can still find time to complain? If we are indulging in complaining, then make no mistake, we are not using our time wisely. If we have time to complain, then we most certainly have time to worship.

Complaining is not only a wrong use of the gift of time God has given us; it is also an exercise that will tie us to our past. *Worship, on the other hand, will connect us to the bright future God has planned for us.*

Complaining caused Israel to be continually tied to Egypt. Had they remembered what the Lord had said and instead used their time in the wilderness to worship Him, it would have positioned them to receive the healing and destiny God desired to give them.

Has Complaining Become a Habit?

Once again at the waters of Marah the Israelite's immediate response to difficulty was this issue called *complaining*, and if we study their history, we see this had become habit for them. They had complained in Egypt, they had complained at the edge of the Red Sea, they had complained at Marah, and they continued to complain once they left Marah.

Make no mistake, left unchecked, complaining can become habit forming, and even addicting in our lives. The good news is bad habits can be broken and replaced with good ones.

If we recognize a habit of complaining in our lives, then it is time to turn it around. One way we can begin to head in that direction is to expose what we are really saying when we complain.

For the Israelites, their complaining took the form of blaming. They turned to Moses and basically said, "You are responsible for our situation! What are *you* going to do about it?" One of the quickest ways to stay right in the middle of our misery is to blame someone else for it.

In his book, *Mastering the Seven Decisions*, Andy Andrews shares this insight:

Who or what do we blame? We blame our parents. We blame the weather. We blame the economy. We blame the president. We blame our spouses. It's amazing who we think of to blame.

Where I am today, we tell ourselves, is a consequence of what other people (our parents, for example) and circumstances have done to me. In blaming other people and events, we weaken our power. We argue, 'It's not my fault...' As soon as we subscribe to this line of thinking, our chances for any kind of success dramatically decline.

When I was at my all-time low – homeless, living under a pier – I remember somebody telling me, 'Well, you chose this.' At first, that infuriated me. I remember thinking, I didn't choose this. If my parents hadn't died, if there had been more insurance, if someone had helped me, if only...

The problem with this line of thinking is that <u>if we don't accept responsibility for where we are right now, we have no hope of changing our future.</u> I promise you: if it's the president's fault, if it's our neighbor's fault, if it's our spouse's fault, if it's the *government's fault, if it's the weather's fault, then we truly are stuck! What are you going to do about the president? What are you going to do about the weather? What can you do about your neighbor? I'll tell you: nothing! But if you can find the answer to your problems in the mirror – if the solution lies within you – well, there's boundless hope, because you can start working on yourself today!* [10]

What alternative to complaining did Israel have? Moses was about to show them. While Israel was complaining and blaming in verse 25 of Exodus 15, Moses' response to the same situation at Marah opens a door for deliverance.

So he cried out to the Lord, and the Lord showed him a tree. When he cast it into the waters the waters were made sweet...

Instead of looking for someone to blame, Moses cried out to God for help and when he did, the answer came. We will explore this lesson more in Chapter Eleven, but notice these verses conclude by telling us that right in middle of all these circumstances the Lord revealed to the people that He was the Lord their Healer. Verse 27 records that from there the people traveled to Elim, which was a place abundant with water and palm trees.

SUMMARY: *The Consequence of a Complaining Response*

When we respond to our circumstances by complaining, we weaken our ability to follow God's guidance for the situation. Complaining also has the ability to tie us to our past and it is one of the quickest ways to stay right in the middle of our misery.

Further Thought

1. What symptoms of "complaining" have you noticed in your everyday life? Are you currently struggling with areas of worry, anxiety, fear, grumbling, or griping?

2. Early on we mentioned the woman in Luke 13 who had a spirit of infirmity. This woman was loosed from her bondage by Jesus, but it is interesting to note that this miracle actually happened in church on the Sabbath Day. In the text it tells us that Jesus called her to come to Him, and when she did she was healed. So what do we see here? We see a woman who was not only in the right place at the right time – in church on the Sabbath – but then she took it a step further by responding to Jesus' call to come closer to Him.

Israel was in the right place at the right time; they had followed God's leading into the wilderness, but then failed to come closer to Him by responding to His call to worship. Maybe you are in the right place at the right time as we speak, but have you answered God's call to you to come closer to Him?

3. Do you know what to do? What has God been prompting you to do as the <u>next step</u> in your situation? I encourage you to write it down and formulate a measureable plan to obey. For instance, if you sense God telling you to read the Bible more, begin by setting a specific time and place to do this. Even if it is a small beginning, a measurable plan will help to overcome the barrier of "good intentions."

✓ 1) Call AT&T – block the #
2) Read this book for clarity
3) Listen to God's prompting for the next step

PART TWO

Overcoming the Crisis

CHAPTER FOUR

A Different Response to Bondage

In 2 Kings 2 we find a very similar situation to compare to that found in Exodus 15, but the key to this comparison is the difference in responses we find.

Look at verses 19 through 22:

> *Then the men of the city said to Elisha, "Please notice, the situation of this city is pleasant, as my lord sees; but the water is bad, and the ground barren." And he said, "Bring me a new bowl, and put salt in it." So they brought it to him. Then he went out to the source of the water, and cast in the salt there, and said, "Thus says the Lord: 'I have healed this water;*

from it there shall be no more death or barrenness." So the water remains healed to this day, according to the word of Elisha which he spoke.

Here again we have a circumstance where a group of people are dealing with bad water, and this water is causing the ground to be barren. This word *barren* in the Hebrew carries with it the idea of *"miscarriage or to make childless."*[11] The implication is that because this ground was unable to produce, various areas of production for the city had been shut down.

Interestingly enough, the city being referred to here is Jericho. Earlier in the Old Testament we are given a little history on Jericho that sheds some light on the problem at hand. Joshua 6:26 reveals that a curse was pronounced on the city by Joshua after Israel had supernaturally conquered it. Looking further into the situation, the Bible tells us that the reason God gave Jericho into the hands of Israel was because of their sins and iniquities. We see this prophesied to Abraham regarding his descendents in Genesis 15:16:

But in the fourth generation they shall return here, for the iniquity of the Amorites is not yet complete.

The term "Amorites" represented all the inhabitants of Canaan, which included Jericho. God was saying there would come a time when their sins and iniquities would be so great the Amorites could no longer be allowed to stay in the land. In Joshua Chapter 6 that time had come. Did Jericho have an opportunity to repent and turn to God? They most certainly did, but only one prostitute named Rahab, along with her family, took this step. As a result, God provided for their deliverance.

Jericho had a history of cursing and maybe like Jericho, we have had cursing in our lives.

We could express the conquering of Jericho this way: "Because of unrepented sins and disobedience to God, Jericho was given over into the hands of their enemies and consequently a curse came upon the city."

A Response of Faith

The previous verses of 2 Kings 19 tell us Elisha, after receiving the mantle of Elijah, struck the waters of the

Jordan River causing them to divide and he walked across on dry ground. The men of Jericho witnessed the event. Here we have the same type of miracle that happened in Exodus. The difference is the Israelites were not just witnesses; *they actually experienced the miracle first hand*! As we compare the two, it becomes evident that though these circumstances were similar, the responses to them were not.

In Exodus, instead of remembering, the Israelites quickly forgot the miraculous deliverance God had just worked in their behalf. Therefore, the minute another difficulty presented itself they easily slipped back into their habit of griping and complaining as if God had never done anything for them.

In 2 Kings 2:19 we see a very different response. The men of the city came to Elisha and presented their problem; however, they did not come to him murmuring and complaining. No, these men came to him in faith as a result of seeing Elisha split the waters of the Jordan River. Instead of forgetting, they responded to this miracle in such a way that belief was stirred up within them.

A Supernatural Request

In verse 20 of 2 Kings Chapter Two, Elisha answers their faith and instructs them to bring him a new bowl containing salt. This was definitely an odd request. Realistically, how are you going to clean up a spring large enough to feed an entire city by using only a bowl containing a little salt? The answer is you are not, at least naturally speaking. No, this was not a natural request. It was a supernatural request and the purpose of it was two-fold.

First, Elisha knew the people needed to be involved with their own deliverance in some way. Bringing the new bowl and salt would serve as an act of obedience for them.

So many times in the Bible we see this principle in action. We are called upon to do what we might view as the "little thing," and when in obedience we do it, God responds by the doing the "big thing." For instance, in James 5:14-15 the sick person is instructed to have the elders of the church pray for him or her, anointing them with oil. In response God heals, and raises up the sick person. In Mark 6:30-44 the disciples were directed to bring a small lunch to Jesus and then to organize people into groups. In response, Jesus multiplied the lunch so five thousand people were miraculously fed. It is amazing, but if we will be faithful to do the seemingly insignificant thing He tells us to, God will do the miracle we can't do.

Secondly, the bowl and salt had a symbolic purpose. As the people acted in obedience to God's command, He would do what they could not do, which was to bring about a spiritual work on the inside of them.

> *Unfortunately the enemy does not care whether we are lazy or ignorant; as long as we are one of the two he will try to take advantage of the situation.*

Let's examine this for a moment. Jericho had a history of cursing and maybe like Jericho, we have had cursing in our lives. This cursing may have come because of the sins and disobedience of others or it could have come from our own past sins and disobedience. Now I am not talking about sins and disobedience we have repented of, but those we have not completely dealt with. These could be areas we may have attempted to deal with, but at some point decided the associated hurt or wound was too painful or overwhelming, so we backed away from them.

Sins and disobedience can only be fully dealt with when we recognize the hurt or wound from which they spring, and then allow God to bring healing to that area. Consider the following sequence of events:

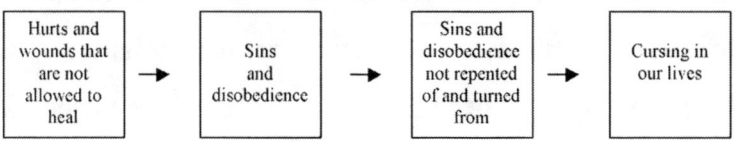

This *backing away* we are describing can be knowing and deliberate or it can be a result of ignorance. Too many times we can be guilty of just wanting the pain to go away therefore, we will seek God only long enough to be free of the present pressure but not long enough to allow Him to heal the source of the pain. Some people do this because of spiritual laziness and others because of spiritual ignorance.

Think of the person who goes to church or reads their Bible just long enough to have their financial situation turned around. Perhaps it was a need in the person's family, their health, or their job that caused them to seek God. However, once the pressure lifted, he or she no longer felt the motivation to pursue a deeper relationship with Him. The truth revealed shows that while God wanted to do a complete work of healing and deliverance in them, they only wanted some momentary relief.

Once the need is met, the spiritually lazy person will find time for everything but God. The spiritually ignorant person will not go on to seek complete healing because he or she does not recognize that Jesus paid the full price to purchase our freedom, our peace, and our restoration. Unfortunately, the enemy does not care whether we are lazy or ignorant; as long as we are one of the two he will try to take advantage of the situation.

Having mentioned spiritual ignorance, we must also be reminded of something we mentioned earlier: *our deliverance is a process*. God told the Israelites He would deliver them little-by-little according to what they could handle at the moment. But *how* would their deliverance come? It would come as they increased in their knowledge of and obedience to the Word of God.

In Exodus 15:26 Moses prophesied to the people that healing would come as they diligently heeded the voice of the Lord and obeyed His commandments. We also read in Joshua 1:8 that when the time came for Joshua to lead Israel as they possessed the promised land, God instructed Joshua that he would need to meditate on God's Word day and night so he could obey everything written in it. In so doing, Joshua and Israel would prosper and have good success.

It is no different for you and me today. James 1:25 calls the Bible, *"The perfect law of liberty"* or we could say "freedom." The more we put God's Word on the inside of us through reading, studying, hearing, meditating, being taught from and obeying it, the more free we will become. Do not be discouraged if you do not have all knowledge of God's Word today! What is important is that you are daily pursuing His Word in a consistent and continual manner. Every step of obedience will bring you closer and closer to complete freedom.

Going Back to the Source

Verse 21 of 2 Kings Chapter Two tells us that the new bowl containing the salt was taken to the "source" of the water. Maybe like this spring that fed throughout the city, our past hurts and wounds have fed into many sectors of our lives causing barrenness, or areas that seem unable to produce.

Examining this condition of barrenness further, Russell Dilday offers this description:

> *A more literal translation would be "and the land casts her young." This seems to suggest that as a*

result of the contaminated spring water, women miscarried, cattle dropped their young prematurely, and trees shed their fruit before it was ripe. [12]

Have you ever found yourself unable to produce something you wanted so badly? Have you ever felt like no matter how hard you tried, you always came up short? Are you lacking real peace, joy, or hope? Do you struggle in areas of insecurity, self-esteem, moodiness, or being able to have good relationships with others? Do you experience constant difficulties in your family, your finances, or your job? Do you find yourself chained to addictions? Have you almost given up on dreams for your future?

Can you see the picture here? Jericho had a water source from which various streams flowed. Trying to treat the situation further down in the streams would do no good because the contamination from the source would continue to flow downstream. Likewise, trying to overcome sins and disobedience in our lives without treating the hurts and wounds from which they stem in our heart can be a futile endeavor.

Let me give a common example: How many times have we thought that our lack of production had to do with the people around us? Maybe we thought we couldn't get ahead or catch any breaks because somehow others were standing in our way or holding us back. If you have experienced this type of perception, then you have probably also noticed that fighting against it is fruitless. Why? Truthfully, it is because no one holds us back but ourselves and the condition of our heart. Streams of insecurity, fear, and resentment will continue to flow out from the source of our heart until we allow God to do a work.

> ***When we finally realize it is more about what is going on between us and God rather than us and other people, we are on our way to real healing.***

We see a real picture of this in 1 Samuel 1. Hannah was one of two wives married to a man by the name of Elkanah. Hannah had no children; she was barren. This was a great hurt in her life that had filtered into her relationships. Her husband did not understand why she could not be content having him alone, and her rival continually provoked her about her inability to conceive, bringing added misery and turmoil to her situation.

Up front, Elkanah could not help Hannah, though he tried, and in the end, Peninnah, her rival, could not hinder her, though she tried. The answer to the bitterness in Hannah's heart was between her and God and no other.

In verse 10 of 1 Samuel 1 we read:

And she was in bitterness of soul, and prayed to the Lord and wept in anguish.

Year after year, Hannah had traveled with her husband to the house of God in Shiloh, but nothing happened to change her misery until the year she cried out to God from the depths of her heart. At that moment, God heard and answered. The bitterness in her heart was healed. Verse 7b says, *"So the woman went her way and ate, and her face was no longer sad."*

Hannah's bitter waters had been made sweet, for she would no longer be barren. The first son she gave birth to would be the prophet Samuel, and in addition *God blessed her with five more children.*

What changed Hannah's barren condition? *She finally realized her true source of supply.*

Back in Exodus, Israel had looked to a natural water source to meet their needs, but God wanted them to look to His supernatural source of supply. When we finally realize that it is more about what is going on between us and God rather than us and other people, we are on our way to real healing.

Streams of Grace

Going back to our analogy, we have stated that the only way a lack of production can be dealt with is to go to the source of the water – if you can change things at the source, you can end the barrenness in other areas.

Psalm 46:4a gives us this beautiful promise:

> *There is a river whose streams shall make glad the city of God...*

Charles Spurgeon expounds on this verse by saying:

> *Divine grace, like a smoothly flowing, fertilizing, full, and never-failing river, yields refreshment and consolation to believers. This is the river of the*

water of life, of which the church above as well as the church below partakes evermore. The streams whereof in their various influences, for they are many, shall make glad the city of God, by assuring the citizens that Zion's Lord will unfailingly supply all their needs. [13]

If we will allow God to come in and heal the contaminated, bitter waters of our heart, and if we will welcome the flow of His divine grace, then we will be amazed at what these living waters can produce in us and in our lives for His glory and for our benefit.

SUMMARY: *A Response of Faith*

When we respond in faith to our circumstances and we obey God's guidance, then we open the door for God to move supernaturally in our situation. In the process of delivering us and cleansing the bitterness of our outward pressure, He will endeavor to cleanse the bitter waters of our heart that led up to it.

Further Thought

1. Are you standing at the River Jordan today? You have opened your eyes to see God's miracles and faith has been stirred in your heart, but now God asks you to do something that doesn't seem reasonable in light of the struggle you are facing. Maybe He is asking you to spend time just worshiping Him. Maybe He is asking you to forget about your circumstance and instead minister to someone else in their difficulty. Maybe He is asking you to volunteer in a certain area of your church.

Whatever He is asking, are you willing to cooperate in your deliverance by obediently bringing your own personal "*new bowl with salt in it*"?

2. In the beginning of the book we made reference to John 8:31-32: *"Then Jesus said to those Jews who believed Him, 'If you abide in My word, you are My disciples indeed. And you shall know the truth, and the truth shall make you free."* The word *know* in verse 32 means *"to understand or to gain knowledge"*[14] and how do we gain knowledge? We gain it by reading, studying, and being taught the Word of God.

In the testimony of the woman who was made straight in Luke 13, we read that her miracle happened after she heard Jesus teaching in the church. What we learn from this is that much of the time teaching comes before deliverance in our lives.

Are you abiding in God's Word today? Are you availing yourself of church and other opportunities to be taught the Word of God? If not, what steps will you take to put the truth of God's Word on the inside of you?

3. Galatians 5:1 gives us this important admonition: *"Stand fast therefore in the liberty by which Christ has made us free, and do not be entangled again with a yoke of bondage."*

This is exactly what happened to Jericho. Five hundred years after Joshua had cursed the city, a man by the name of Hiel of Bethel (1 Kings 16:34) tried to rebuild it at the expense of his oldest and youngest sons; exactly what Joshua had said would happen. But even in the midst of revisited bondage, God still had a plan of deliverance for this city once they cried out to Him in faith.

Maybe you are one who has experienced the liberating power of God only to return once again to the same bondage. If that is so, be encouraged today; God still has a plan for your deliverance if you will only cry out to Him in faith.

CHAPTER FIVE

Taking the Time to Deal with Bondage

Have you ever heard someone say, "Just leave the past in the past"? Certainly there is some truth to this statement, because when we talk about dealing with our past, we are not advocating digging up a bunch of sordid details; if we are not careful, doing so could be opening up an old wound rather than pursuing a path that will allow it to completely heal. What we are talking about is understanding there are issues in our life that need to be recognized, acknowledged, repented of if need be, and then fully given to God. Once we do this, we can then press into the things of God so He can begin to strengthen that previously weak area.

At this point we could use the classic example of a person who has been married several times and divorced as many. We could ask, "Who is the common denominator here?" And the answer would be, "This person." Unless they stop long enough to fully deal with why these divorces happened-from their own part of the equation-then they are doomed to repeat the same mistakes over and over again. The person, who avoids this process and only looks for another relationship to cover the pain, in the end, will never be really free of the pain.

God is not only intimately involved with our present circumstances; He is also concerned with our future.

In John Chapter Four, Jesus counseled the woman at the well concerning her heart in light of the fact that she had been married five times. Jesus explained that each of her marriages had left her still thirsting, but if she would turn to Him and let Him do a healing work in her, she would find the Water Source that would cause her *never* to thirst again.

What is the application to our lives in the challenges we are presently experiencing? How are we to understand this continual thirsting? Consider this: if we don't face up to and deal with the hurts and wounds from our past, but instead we cover them over and just move on or run away, then every time we are put in that type of situation again we may unknowingly find ourselves responding out of that old wound. This type of response will cause us to be forever drinking, but never able to quench the real thirsting in our heart.

Once they left Marah, did Israel face more "water" issues? Yes. Did they respond in the same unbelieving way each time? Yes, but each of these episodes could have been very different had they stopped long enough the first time to question why they were stumbling in their ability to trust God, and long enough to look at the real state of their heart.

In Psalm 139:23-24 the Psalmist prayed:

Search me, O God, and know my heart; Try me, and know my anxieties; and see if there is any wicked way in me, and lead me in the way everlasting.

Letting God Search *My* Heart

A number of years ago, before I was married, I experienced the painful breakup of a relationship. In retrospect, I now realize that even though I sought God about it at the time, and allowed Him to do some real changing in my heart, I didn't have enough understanding to let Him do a complete work. Now fast forward a few years later; I found myself dealing with the breakup of another relationship; however, because this relationship was far less serious in nature than the first, I was surprised at how emotionally devastated I felt over it.

It was at this juncture that God brought me to our study on Exodus 15 and 2 Kings 2. As I meditated on these passages of scripture, I finally realized I had to stop and take the time needed to allow God to completely heal and restore my heart. It was a process, but one that prepared me for the *right* man God would eventually bring into my life; the man I am happily married to today.

How do you know if it is time to stop and pursue God's healing work in your heart? Let me ask you: Have you ever had something happen to you resulting in a big emotional response, and maybe afterwards you thought, "What is the deal? Why am I so upset or fearful about this?" If you are alert to recognizing this type of wake-up call, then it is time to stop and allow God to search your heart and to begin His healing process.

I recently heard a pastor say, *"Whatever God reveals, He wants to heal."* [15]

Out with the Old, in with the New

God is not only intimately involved with our present circumstances; He is also concerned with our future. Jeremiah 29:11 declares that God has made plans to give us a future devoid of evil and filled with hope. He goes on to say in verse 13 that this becomes possible when we begin to search for God with all our heart. *"All our heart"* implies we give all of the hurts and wounds in our heart to Him.

Second Kings 2 provides further insight into God's plan for our future. In verse 20 Elisha told them to bring him a new bowl with salt in it. The new bowl represented the new thing God wanted to do in their lives; in fact, one commentary put it this way:

Elisha's miracle fully removed the age-old judgment, thus allowing a new era to dawn on this area. [16]

We need to understand that God wants a "new era" to dawn in our lives, right now, right where we live.

But in order for this new era to dawn, we must look at the second half of this equation, which was what the salt represented: *purification*. One property of salt is that it can act as a purifier; what is it that needs to be purified? The answer would be our past hurts and wounds; those things that have allowed cursing to come into our lives. The reason this purification is so essential is that it wouldn't do God any good to bring a new thing into our life if we were still responding to it out of old hurts and wounds.

Isaiah 43:18-19 puts it this way:

Do not remember the former things, nor consider the things of old. Behold I will do a new thing, now it shall spring forth; shall you not know it? I will even make a road in the wilderness and rivers in the desert.

Do you see that this new thing God desires to do will happen as we forget or "let go" of the former things? Once we have faced and dealt with the past, with God's help it is now time to forget the past. Where there has formerly been a wilderness and a desert, there will now be a new path and rivers of refreshing.

Let's take a closer look at this statement, *"I will make a road in the wilderness and rivers in the desert."* If a person is in the wilderness or desert, it is very easy to be completely lost, to wander about and to never find your way out. If, however, you come upon a road or a river, you can simply follow its path out every time. As you press into God, He is going to show you the road that will lead you out, and He will provide the rivers of refreshing and the provision you will need along the way.

> *Where there has been a wilderness and a desert, there will now be a new path and rivers of refreshing.*

If we apply the phrase "road in the wilderness" to our study at hand, we will see that it also indicates we will need to go in a new direction of response if we are going to be free of bondages in our life. For instance, once we make a decision to begin crying out to God for deliverance, the complaining also needs to stop.

Leviticus 26:10 gives this instruction: *"You shall eat the old harvest, and clear out the old because of the new."*

Once we get on this new road of response we will find that God has a great destination planned for us. Back in 2 Kings 2:21-22 we are told that once the waters of Jericho were healed or purified at the source, they remained healed permanently. There would be no more death and no more barrenness. Could we have better news than this? How would you like to have a change or deliverance in some area of your life that was so complete, it was permanent? This complete work is exactly what God wants to do on the inside of us as we cooperate with Him in bringing needed healing to our heart, which is the source of every spring flowing in our life.

Keep your heart with all diligence, for out of it spring the issues of life. Proverbs 4:23

SUMMARY: *Recognizing the Connection to the Past*

In order to have real healing we must understand that many times our response has a history; it is tied to the hurts and wounds of our past. God desires to purify that history and to give us a new response that will lead us into the hope-filled future He has planned for us.

Further Thought

1. In Psalm 139:19-24, the Psalmist is stirred up in his emotions because of the wicked men around him and the enemies he is facing. Finally, he shifts his focus off of these people and onto himself and his own heart before God. He cries out, "*Search me, O God, and know my heart…see if there is any wicked way in me.*" Ultimately he knew the only real answer would come from first letting God do a work in *his* heart.

Is it time for you to shift your focus off of the people and the circumstances around you and onto the work God wants to do in your heart?

2. Even if your situation today seems like a wilderness or a desert, God has provided a road leading out. First Corinthians

10:13 tells us that with every temptation we face, God has already provided a way of escape. One key to positioning ourselves to recognize this escape route is to make sure our response to the pressure we are experiencing is in line with God's Word.

Do you need a new direction of response? Do you need to turn in the direction of forgiveness, humility, obedience, finally putting your trust in God, or making a decision to walk in His peace?

3. Once we change directions, as Proverbs 4:23 admonishes, we will need to "*Keep* (guard or protect) *our heart*" from anything that would get us off track. One way we can guard our heart is to daily keep it bathed in the Word of God and prayer. The Bible also talks about the importance of the company we keep, as well as what we allow our eyes to see and our ears to hear.

What are you actively doing in an effort to guard or protect your heart?

- Recognize/acknowledge the stronghold of all these years
- Resist that temptation
- Confess my sin
- Repent and turn around & go the other way

CHAPTER SIX

The Signs of Bondage – Part 1

In 2 Kings 2, the city of Jericho was able to receive healing because the inhabitants recognized they had a definite problem. Without this realization no one would have sought healing, and therefore, the bad water would have continued to flow. It is the same for us: *no healing can come until we recognize the signs of a problem.*

The Israelites had only to look at the location of their crisis to begin to see signs of a problem in their lives. Just like Jericho, the Wilderness of Shur had a history and a story to tell.

So Moses brought Israel from the Red Sea; then they went out into the Wilderness of Shur. Exodus 15:22

Names in the Old Testament quite frequently carry a great deal of meaning, and the name "Shur" is no exception. Its' meaning is very significant having three parts to its definition[17]:

- A wall
- A fort or fortified city
- Vision or to look around

Each of these definitions will give us specific insight into what was going on behind the scenes in the verses of Exodus 15, and we will examine them one at a time.

To begin with, the name "Shur" can mean a "wall." When we think of a wall, we picture something that divides, separates, surrounds, or encloses. Walls have the ability to hem us in while keeping others out, and they most certainly are a product of bondage.

> *The building of a "wall" happens in the heart as a reaction to a hurt or wound that is not totally given to God.*

Let me ask you, "Have you ever felt like there was a wall in some part of your life that you couldn't seem to break through?" Maybe you have struggled with feelings of jealousy, insecurity, fear, or guilt. Quite possibly you have been aware of the seeming barrier and even frustrated that you have been unable to make progress beyond it.

Up front we must understand that the building of a "wall" happens in the heart as a reaction to a hurt or wound that has not been totally given to God.

One reason "walls" can shut down progress in our lives is they have the ability to control us. If allowed to remain, they can control our sense of self-worth, our sense of security, and even the level of peace and joy we can experience. Make no mistake; walls in our lives will manipulate how we react to circumstances in life as well as how much personal growth is possible for us.

Let's begin by examining some signs that will help you to recognize if there are any "walls" in your life from the past.

Walls Can Hinder Our Believing

Belief is essential to the Christian life. It is through believing that we are:

- Born again (John 1:12; 3:36)
- Recipients of answered prayer (Mark 11:23-24)
- Enabled to overcome fear (Mark 5:36)
- Enabled to enter into the works of God (John 6:28-29)

When our ability to believe God is hindered in any way, whether in a particular area of our lives or altogether, it greatly limits His ability to help us and to bring the healing we need. Our inability to believe can be tied to any number of areas including:

- Resentment toward God over circumstances from our past
- Fear that dominates our mind
- Lack of understanding of God's Word regarding the "process" of deliverance
- Succumbing to discouragement
- Focusing on the difficulties we are experiencing

Belief in the goodness of God to help us is something that should come naturally to the believer; however, "walls" in our life can shut down our production and progress in this portion of our Christian walk. This inability to believe God is a sign alerting us to the fact that walls from the past exist that must come down, but accomplishing this will require a change in focus.

Focusing on *Wonders* Rather than *Wounds*

In the case of the Israelites, we have seen that the bitter waters of Marah revealed a "wall" of unbelief. When the reality of the situation became apparent, and if they had been responding with a mindset of belief, they would have said, "What is this little bit of water to our God who just split an entire sea in two?"

This should have been the obvious reaction. After all, three days before, these people had been in the middle of one of the most spectacular miracles ever known to mankind. Yet, when they found themselves facing another problem involving the same substance-*water*-they totally lost sight of what they had just witnessed and experienced.

Vividly, God had miraculously displayed that dealing with water was not impossible for Him; in fact, He displayed that He was Lord and Ruler over the water, but these people could not see it. In essence they were blinded to it because they were still viewing everything through the eyes of their past hurts and wounds and could not comprehend that this was just another opportunity to watch God work in their behalf.

Like so many people today, the Israelites were "going under" in the midst of their circumstances because they were focused on their past *wounds* instead of the past *wonders* God had performed in their lives. The Psalmist had a revelation of the power of remembering God's past wonders and in Psalm 77:2-14 he came to this conclusion:

In the day of my trouble I sought the Lord...I remembered God, and was troubled; I complained, and my spirit was overwhelmed...And I said, "This is my anguish; but I will remember the years of the right hand of the Most High." I will remember the works of the Lord; surely I will remember Your wonders of old. I will also meditate on all Your work, and talk of Your deeds. Your way, O God, is in the sanctuary; who is so great a God as our God? You are the God who does wonders; You have declared Your strength among the peoples.

What were the *wounds* that Israel focused on rather than the *wonders* God had done for them? Their wounds came from the bondage and mistreatment they had experienced in Egypt. Some have accurately stated, "God may have delivered the Israelites out of Egypt, but he couldn't get Egypt out of them." As a result, these particular people never entered into the Promised Land, which was the "new thing" God had for them.

The Israelites were "going under" in the midst of their circumstances because they were focused on their past wounds instead of the past wonders God had performed in their lives.

They had cried and groaned and complained in Egypt, and no matter how many times they saw God move in their behalf, the moment they encountered another difficulty in the wilderness they immediately reverted back to their old behavior. This brings us to a key point. As we read through the Bible we see that God delivered the Israelites out of crisis after crisis, *but because they wouldn't change on the inside, He couldn't bring them into the permanent deliverance He had for them on the outside*, which again for them, was the Promised Land.

You see, you are not going to have deliverance without change. Something must change on the inside at the level of our heart. God was trying to do a new thing in their lives, but they would abort and squelch it every time by their response. It is the same for us; in order for God's plan to be fully birthed in our lives, God's new thing must be met by our new response.

What did we see with Jericho? Once they met their crisis with a new response, not only to their difficulty but also to the miracle they witnessed, their city was no longer barren. Remember, Isaiah told us that the new thing would not be like the former things.

Focusing on the Deliverer Rather than the Disappointment

Let's look at an example of this inability to believe from the New Testament:

And when He came to the disciples, He saw a great multitude around them, and scribes disputing with them. Immediately, when they saw Him, all the people were greatly amazed, and running to Him, greeted Him. And He asked the scribes, "What are you discussing with them?" Then one of the crowd answered and said, "Teacher, I brought You my son, who has a mute spirit. And whenever it seizes him, it throws him down; he foams at the mouth, gnashes his teeth, and becomes rigid. So I spoke to Your disciples, that they should cast it out, but they could not." He answered him and said, "O faithless generation, how long shall I be with you? How long shall I bear with you? Bring him to Me." Then they brought him to Him. And when he saw Him, immediately the spirit convulsed him, and he fell on the ground and wallowed, foaming at the mouth. So He asked his father, "How long has this been happening to him?" And he said, "From childhood. And often he has thrown him both into the fire and into the water to destroy him. But if You can do anything, have compassion on us and help us." Jesus said to him, "f you can believe, all things are possible to him who believes." Immediately the father of the child cried out and said with tears, "Lord, I believe, help my unbelief!" Mark 9:14-24

Here we are told about a man who had a son who suffered from demonic seizures since he was a child, and many times these seizures would throw him into the fire and into the water in an attempt to burn and drown him. It was awful, and what we see from this is that sometimes people can have hurts and wounds just because they have been through so much. We can readily understand that this would have caused great suffering in a family. In fact, in circumstances like these, over time people can develop a fear of ever letting themselves hope again; it is a wall of discouragement that has gone up in their lives hindering their ability to believe God for an answer.

Looking at these scriptures, we could blame the disciples for not being able to cast this demonic torment out of the boy, but could there have been another factor holding back deliverance as well? Could it also have been that because of "walls" in this father's life, he was having difficulty believing? We really get a hint of this possibility when Jesus addresses the man and gives this insight: "If *you* can believe, all things are possible to him who believes."

In response, the father immediately cried out, "I believe, help thou my unbelief." The father demonstrated he was ready to change, and we are told he went away with his son completely healed.

Instead of being manipulated by walls of fear and discouragement, *this man changed his response to his circumstance by putting his trust in Jesus and when he did, God was able to bring about a new thing in his life.*

The Walls of the Heart

As we look at the connection between "walls" and believing, we once again turn to the comparison we have been observing. The city of Jericho and the Wilderness of Shur are the two backdrops in which we find a problem with water followed by divine answers to each dilemma. In one situation we have bad water and in the other bitter, but both bring about a crisis that must be dealt with.

Both Jericho and the Wilderness of Shur had a history of "walls." In contrast to the rebuilt Jericho found in 2 Kings 2, the Jericho of old also witnessed a miracle crossing at the Jordan River. Joshua 3:14-17 gives this account,

> *So it was, when the people set out from their camp to cross over the Jordan, with the priests bearing the*

ark of the covenant before the people, and as those who bore the ark came to the Jordan, and the feet of the priests who bore the ark dipped in the edge of the water (for the Jordan overflows all its banks during the whole time of harvest), that the waters which came down from upstream stood still, and rose in a heap very far away at Adam, the city that is beside Zaretan. So the waters that went down into the Sea of the Arabah, the Salt Sea, failed, and were cut off; and the people crossed over opposite Jericho. Then the priests who bore the ark of the covenant of the Lord stood firm on dry ground in the midst of the Jordan; and all Israel crossed over on dry ground, until all the people had crossed completely over the Jordan.

At this juncture, Jericho had an opportunity to respond in faith to the miracle God displayed right in front of them. But as mentioned earlier, only one woman, Rahab, chose to open her heart to God, and as a result she and her family were saved. The rest of Jericho chose the opposite and Joshua 6:1 gives a vivid picture of the state of their hardened hearts:

Now Jericho was securely shut up because of the children of Israel; none went out, and none came in.

In fear, the people of Jericho trusted in their walls to protect them when time of judgment came and the walls fell down flat. Did they have a history of sin, rebellion, unbelief and hurt? Absolutely, but a response of faith could have changed everything for them and for their future. Sadly that did not happen.

Yes, Jericho knew about walls; however, many years later they would also come to know about God's restoring power. Because the men of Jericho would finally come to a place of believing, we find in Nehemiah 3:2 that they would even eventually help to rebuild the walls of the restored Jerusalem.

Faith was also missing in the Israelites at Marah in the Wilderness of Shur. Their fear and complaining displayed that they had essentially shut up the walls of their hearts toward God. When we do this, we lose our ability to hear from God and to see what He needs to show us for the situation at hand.

SUMMARY: *Stopping the Flow of Negative Response*

Once bondage is exposed, it must be recognized for what it is. Life hindering, unproductive responses will continue to flow until we learn to recognize the signs of bondage. The most evident sign is when a person continually struggles to believe even after seeing the miracles.

Further Thought

1. At the beginning of this chapter we made reference to Mark 5:36. There Jairus, a ruler of the synagogue, was confronted with great fear. His daughter was dying, but while he went to get Jesus, some people came running to tell him it was too late; his daughter was dead. Immediately Jesus turned to him and said, "*Do not be afraid, only believe.*" But how could he continue to believe in the face of such a report?

The Psalmist declared in Psalm 56:3, "*Whenever I am afraid, I will trust in You.*" It is possible to trust God when we are overwhelmed with great fear when we understand that fear is an emotion, but trust and belief arise from an act of our will. The good news is our will, when put into action, is always stronger than our emotions; it will prevail and bring us through to victory just like it did for Jairus. His obedient act to believe God, even in the midst of fear, brought healing and resurrection to his daughter.

Do you have "walls" of fear in your life today that have convinced you they are stronger than your ability to believe? If so, I challenge you to make a decision to believe regardless. As you do, your "walls" of fear will begin to crumble and fall.

2. What "wounds" do you need to quit focusing on and what "wonders" do you need to remember?

3. Is there an area of your life in which you have shut up the walls of your heart toward God? If it feels like there is a wall you cannot seem to get beyond in your relationship with Him, it could be that *you* have to let the walls down. James 4:8b gives us direction: *"Draw near to God and He will draw near to you."* Are you willing to make the first move in drawing near to God? He is there waiting for you.

CHAPTER SEVEN

The Signs of Bondage – Part 2

We saw in the last chapter that "walls" are a product of bondage and can actually hinder our ability to believe God for the freedom and deliverance we need. Now we will look at a second sign indicating there could be a wall from the past in our life.

Have you ever found yourself continually overreacting to a particular set of circumstances? Stepping out of the wounds of the past to live our lives forward will require a thoughtful look at this question. Some examples of these overreactions could include:

- Becoming easily offended
- Becoming easily angered

- A tendency toward jealousy or envy
- Moodiness or depression
- Becoming easily intimidated or fearful
- Having an unrealistic need to please people
- Perfectionism
- Rebellion

Growing up I had numerous challenges with fear. To this day my family still teases me about the times I would go crazy with fear over situations even as small as having a splinter in my finger! (It's embarrassing, but true!) It certainly is funny now, but as a child I can still remember the feelings of terror I would experience over anything having to do with pain, doctors, or hospitals. You want to talk about overreacting! Many times it was just ridiculous.

Not too long ago it finally dawned on me that the root of this fear was possibly something that happened to me when I was five years old. My parents had taken a little vacation leaving my brother and me with family. While they were gone, there was a terrible car accident that claimed the life of my grandmother and threatened to claim the life of my brother who was three at the time.

By the miracle-working power of God and much prayer, my brother lived but was in the hospital for quite a while. At five years old, this was a lot for me to take in and emotionally process. I believe much of the fear I experienced later in life perhaps started at this time.

Overcoming this tendency to overreact with fear took time because it had filtered into other areas of my life as well. I not only battled fear with all things medical, I also experienced fear in many social situations coupled with extreme shyness. In addition, I struggled with fears of failure and having the confidence to step out in areas of personal growth. As you can imagine, all of this hindered me in making significant progress in my life.

At this point you might ask, "Rhonda, how can you really be sure that all the fear started with the accident?" Quite honestly, I can't be sure, but at least it gives me some measure of understanding to build upon. Truthfully, the more important question I want to discuss is *how did I overcome this paralyzing wall of fear?* The short answer is simply with God's help I faced it.

The biggest asset I had going for me as a child and a teenager was that I knew Jesus; I was born again. I didn't have a great amount of teaching from God's Word at that time in my life, but I did know enough to pray and talk to God when I needed help.

As I approached the end of my senior year of high school, I was still deciding what to do after graduation. When people asked me what my plans were, I only felt confident of what I was sure I would *not* do! My quick answer was, "I am still deciding, but I do know it will *not* be anything to do with the medical field!"

> ***As I began to face present day fears head on, the terror of the past started to subside.***

Little did I know, God was about to lead me into a situation that would start the process of breaking the fear off of my life. That spring my aunt, a nurse, learned about a special program at the hospital where she worked. It was a school to train x-ray technicians, and she immediately realized what a great educational opportunity it was. Excited, she brought an application home for me. Not wanting to disappoint my aunt, I filled it out; however, I still had no intention of heading in that direction.

In the process of applying, I learned only fifteen students for the following school year would be selected. Once I had made it through all the interviews, the fact that I was told over six hundred people had applied coupled with the realization that I didn't have some of the required classes in my background, caused me not to give the whole possibility a second thought. That is, except for the fact that my mother and I had prayed for God's direction concerning it. To my great surprise, two days later I had an acceptance letter in the mail. I knew it had to be the hand of God, and so that fall I entered x-ray school.

Though I struggled the first few months and even came very close to quitting, I put all my efforts into my studies. That along with much prayer and reliance on God caused me to be one of the top students in my graduating class. The first layer of fear in my life had begun to peel off.

As a student in x-ray, I was introduced to every aspect of a county hospital including the morgue, surgery, and many hours in the emergency room. These were big hurdles for me to overcome, but instead of backing down, each time I made the choice to face the hurdles and allow God to help me.

Along the way the fear of failure began to loosen its hold on me as well. I realized with God's help I *could* finish, I *could* accomplish and do well. Over the years, working in the medical field caused me to be less and less fearful of many of the things that had previously tormented me growing up.

In the midst of all this progress, I also began to realize that the hurt of the original trauma started to heal. For years, even into my twenties, I was unable to talk about what had happened without a sense of panic and terror overcoming me. Periodically relatives would come over and nostalgic conversations would head in that direction. Each time I would quietly leave the room unable to listen at all. But eventually as I began to face present day fears head on, I noticed that the terror of the past started to subside until I could finally look back upon the event in a healthy way, acknowledging what happened but no longer overwhelmed with the emotional hurt of it.

Facing Hurts and Wounds

Freedom from our past means we must face the hurts and wounds found there, but lasting healing can only come when we face these things in God and with His help and direction. Let me give you an example to illustrate this.

When I was twenty-nine years old, I experienced another traumatic incident. While out walking one summer morning in a residential neighborhood, I was attacked by two Chow dogs. The short version of this story is God miraculously delivered me. The long version is it happened during the week when most people are working; therefore, by the time help arrived on the scene I was in a dire situation. The dogs had knocked me on my back and were very close to my neck. I ended up with ten puncture wounds and a serious laceration to my arm.

There is no doubt God protected me and after a number of stitches I started the process of healing, physically, that is. Mentally and emotionally it was another story. That very night I began to have nightmares and great apprehension about leaving my apartment because someone in my building owned a Chow dog that was not always kept on a leash.

Somehow, in this particular area, I had lost my ability to distinguish between the past and the present.

A couple of days later, a friend suggested I go right back out and start walking again in the hope that by doing so I would conquer any lingering fear.

The next morning I headed out determined to face the fear of what had happened to me. However, it wasn't long before

I heard a front door open releasing a large black dog headed directly toward me. I literally panicked. Its owner simply laughed as the dog jumped all over me. In the past I would have been nothing more than annoyed over the thoughtlessness of this person, but once again I felt paralyzed by fear. It was definitely an overreaction to the situation. The dog, though large, was obviously of the friendly sort, but my fear could not discern that enough to give me comfort.

From that day on I struggled with a fear of dogs. Big dogs, little dogs, friendly dogs, it didn't matter; they all brought up the feelings of the terror I felt the day I had been attacked. Somehow, in this particular area, I had lost my ability to distinguish between the past and the present. Obviously, the vast majority of dogs I would encounter from that point on would not be out to harm me, but explain that to my emotions! Most definitely, another wall of fear had been erected in my life.

Leaning on God and His Word

Even though God had protected me outwardly in the dog attack, I still needed to learn about receiving His inward healing and protection. Leaning on His Word like never before would be a key to this lesson.

Approximately five years after I was attacked by dogs, I had a third "traumatic" event occur in my life. I had just arrived home one evening from getting a few groceries. It was after dark and as I emerged from my car, grocery bag and purse in hand, I didn't pay attention to the fact that one of the overhead lights had gone out in my apartment parking lot.

I had made it halfway up the walk to where I lived when I heard someone calling out to me. As I turned, I realized it was a young man in a car asking for directions. In the dim light I mistook him for a new resident in my building. Naively I walked back closer to his car giving him time to get out and come around to my side.

The next thing I knew there was a gun in my face as the young man demanded my purse. Quite honestly I panicked and threw everything in my arms onto the pavement between us. As I backed away, he grabbed my purse and took off. Thankfully, I still had my apartment keys in hand and I quickly went into my apartment and called the police.

It was quite an evening as the police arrived, and I learned that this young man was in the middle of a robbery spree. He had already robbed several people before me. The good news was I became the last successful robbery. Shortly after calling the police, I called my family and we prayed. God caused the young man's next attempt to be foiled and the final attempt was on someone who recognized him, shutting his evening down altogether! Two days later he was in jail, and months later he was headed to prison.

Simply facing the hurt or the wound will not set you free unless you do it leaning on the power of God and the promises in His Word.

The night of the robbery I had two people offer to spend the night with me, concerned I possibly had been carrying a second key to my apartment in the stolen purse. I decided to face the night alone. What happened next was a very significant learning experience for me in my walk as a Christian.

At this point in my life I had learned a little more about dealing with fear. I certainly did not want fear in this situation to take hold of me like the dog attack incident had done. Therefore, I sat down at my kitchen table and opened my Bible. I began to read scriptures on God's promise of protection. I also had a tape of scripture put to music. One song in particular focused on Luke 10:19 where Jesus said, *"Behold, I give you authority to trample on serpents and scorpions, and over all the power of the enemy, and nothing shall by any means hurt you."*

I must have played this scripture song at least 30 times. The more I played it and sang along, the more I entered into God's peace. I kept playing it until I knew I was free of any fear. I went to bed that night and slept great. In the days to follow, even though I had to go through several questionings by the police, picture line ups, and court related issues, I never had one bad dream or moment of fearful feelings.

The difference between the dog attack and robbery was amazing. When I look back on the robbery, from the beginning it always felt like it happened to someone else rather than me. I just had no anxiety concerning it. What I learned from these incidents is that it is not enough to merely face your past or your fears. In both instances I endeavored to do that, but the first time around it only seemed to dig me deeper into the pit of fear.

Simply facing the hurt or the wound will not set you free unless you do it leaning on the power of God and the promises in His Word. When I did this after the robbery, complete freedom and healing came.

Distinguishing Between Past and Present

Have you found yourself unable to emotionally distinguish between past and present in certain areas of your life? If so, this is a huge signpost of bondage from our past. Do you find yourself becoming angry, fearful, jealous, resentful or impatient in measures all out of proportion to the reality of what really is happening in present? Let's consider some examples:

- One lady I know experienced a circumstance of infidelity in a previous marriage. After she remarried she found herself overwhelmed with fear whenever her husband had to work late. She shared with me that each time this would happen she would pace back and forth in their driveway waiting for him to arrive, all the while frantic that he might be cheating on her. Finally, one night she realized she had to make a decision: "Either I trust God with my marriage or I don't, but I cannot go on like this." Once she decided to face her present situation with faith in God regardless of what had happened to her in the past, she was set free. Today, many years later, she continues to enjoy a happy and secure marriage.

- I have counseled other people who have experienced tremendous fear and anxiety in the present because of loss in the past. Having experienced the death of a loved one in the past, they fight constant fear that something will happen to someone close to them in the present.

- I have also known many people who struggle with present relationships because of hurts they experienced in the past concerning their parents. Maybe a parent was very distant or uninvolved, disapproving or even absent altogether.

Whatever the circumstance might be, when we overreact or blow things out of proportion, it may very well be that the present situation is bringing up old feelings from an old wound that has not been allowed to completely heal. What is the answer to this dilemma?

Identifying the True Source or Your Emotions

We have talked about facing these things in God's strength and with His help, but I also believe a little understanding can go a long way.

When you have overblown feelings of fear, anger, insecurity, offense, or whatever the emotion might be, it is important to acknowledge they are *real feelings*. The trauma or difficult circumstance you went through created these emotions in you. Understand then, that when certain "trigger" situations happen in the present they can cause those emotions to resurface. However, you must identify and remember that these emotions are tied to the past and have nothing to do with the present reality. Having done that, you can now look at these objectively and say, "I know who you are, and I know you are *not* about today, so I am going to take you and set you over *here.*" You might even call this compartmentalizing. Once you have put these emotions in their proper context, you can then deal with your present circumstances and are better able to trust God and walk in wisdom concerning the situation.

Each time you approach a present difficulty this way, you will find that more healing comes. Putting things in their proper perspective allows you to appropriately deal with the reality of the present while leaving more and more of the past behind and embracing a new future in God.

Overblown emotions that control our response to situations are definitely a sign that there is a wall in our life that needs to come down, but the good news here is that the God we serve is in the wall removal business!

SUMMARY: *Considering the Emotional Link to Our Past*

Our emotions, or feelings, can hold clues to the bondages in our life. If our emotional reactions are out of proportion to the actual circumstances we face, then it is likely they have more to do with our past than our present.

Further Thought

1. In the book of 1 Samuel we find the account of Saul being anointed as the first king of Israel. When the prophet Samuel told Saul of this calling, Saul responded by questioning how this could be since his family was from the tribe of Benjamin, the smallest of all the tribes (1 Samuel 9:20-21). Benjamin was the smallest tribe because it had a history of rebellion and disobedience to God and as a result, was almost wiped out at one point (Judges 19; 20).

Not long into his reign, this same spirit of rebellion began to surface in Saul. When David later came on the scene as one of his army commanders (1 Samuel 18:5), Saul was overwhelmed with jealousy and resentment toward him because of his success. These emotions soon turned into moodiness and depression. Saul had many opportunities to face his negative emotions head on and to turn in a direction of freedom, but each time he instead clung to his wall of resentment. In the end this wall proved to be his downfall.

Is there an overwhelming negative emotion in your life you have clung to? Saul's negative emotions only pointed to the real bondage on the inside of him which was a spirit of rebellion. Ask God to show you what real heart issue is tied to the negative emotion in your life.

2. Do you have areas of bondage in your life you have tried to face on your own? How can you begin to instead, lean on God and His Word in these areas?

3. Early in David's life we see a confident, assertive young man, who is zealous for the things of God. Over time he begins to experience some wounds: Rejection from his family, Saul's jealousy and resentment that turned into life-threatening attacks, and a wife who is taken from him and given to another man (1 Samuel 25:44). Gradually he begins to take multiple wives in direct violation of God's command for a king (Deuteronomy 17:17), he commits adultery and murder, and instead of the former confidence and assertive-

ness, he becomes a king who rules his family and nation with indecisiveness, complacency, and many times, weakness.

Could David's immoral actions, indecisiveness, and complacency have been an overreaction to the hurts of his past? Though David continued to serve God, we see indications in his later life that he had not allowed wounds of rejection, personal attack, and deception to completely heal.

Do you have current areas in your life that could be an overreaction to the wounds of the past? Can you begin to identify the associated feelings and work to put them in their proper perspective?

4. Sometimes we can be blind toward our own overreactions; therefore, if we really desire to take steps toward freedom, we will consider what others are telling us. It will take boldness, but ask yourself, "What do other people say I overreact to?" With an open heart discuss the answer to this question with the Lord. The resulting insight and revelation could bring about a turning point in your situation.

CHAPTER EIGHT

The Signs of Bondage – Part 3

In the last two chapters we have examined two signs that let us know there are walls in our lives from the past stemming from bondage. We have also talked about the controlling effect these walls have in our lives. However, there is still a third sign we need to examine.

Have you ever just felt overwhelmed by your circumstances; I mean feeling overwhelmed to the point of being unable to act in a reasonable manner?

The Bible definition of the word *overwhelmed* is *"to be feeble, to faint or to grow weak."* *"It can pertain to either physical exhaustion or the languishing of man's innermost being."*[18] It is the picture of a person who is covered over with darkness.[19]

This feeling of having "too much to carry" is most likely due to the "past" you are dragging along behind you.

David's Example

There are four times in the book of Psalms where David describes himself as being overwhelmed by his circumstances (Psalm 61:2, 77:3, 142:3 and 143:4). Each time, however, we see him climb up out of this weakened state of darkness as he cries out to God for help and as he remembers God's goodness and miracle-working power from the past.

David was not perfect and he certainly had a past that had produced hurts and wounds, but his God-given genius was the ability to rise above his fainting emotions to fulfill his purpose in God.

Anyone can be temporarily overwhelmed by the pressures of life, but when we allow ourselves to become overwhelmed to the point that progress is impeded, it is a sure sign a wall exists in our life.

This sign usually manifests when we experience mounting stress. As long as circumstances are not too difficult and we feel like we still have control, we can coast along. But as soon as the pressure increases or one circumstance too many is thrown into the mix, the walls of anger, depression, offense, low self-esteem, or fear are exposed. Immediately, we shut down mentally and emotionally and fail to deal with whatever the situation is in a rational manner.

> ## *God is never your problem; He is always your answer.*

For example, a man once shared with me that he battles feelings of resentment toward God because of hurts from his past; however, this resentment does not usually surface until the pressures of life reach a certain point. When things seemingly get too difficult in particular areas, feelings of God's perceived unfairness begin to flood him. From then on he finds himself struggling to climb out of a pit of depression. Because of this wall of resentment in his life, he never seems to be able to progress beyond a certain level.

In 2 Chronicles 20, King Jehoshaphat (King of Judah) found himself facing this kind of pressure, yet, he took an approach that led him to deliverance rather than being dragged under by the circumstances and the fear he felt.

In verse 2 he was told that a great multitude of armies had banded together against Judah and these armies were headed in their direction. This would definitely go under the heading of "one too many things," and yet, instead of succumbing to overwhelming feelings of panic, the people set themselves to seek God.

Their cry for help consisted of three things: *remembering and acknowledging how great God was, recounting the past miracles He had performed for them,* and *a humble plea for guidance.* This faith-filled response to their circumstances laid a foundation for a miraculous victory on their behalf. In answer to their cry, God declared He would fight the battle for them, which is exactly what happened. On the following day, as they headed out praising and worshipping God, they discovered that their enemies had been self-slaughtered. Each of the enemy armies had turned one upon another.

As King Jehoshaphat discovered, there is encouragement for the overwhelmed person. When the stresses of life seem too great and feelings of resentment, guilt, fear, shame, or depression try to overflow you, there is one thing you can be sure of: *God is never your problem; He is always your answer.*

Encouraging Ourselves

In the end, the overwhelmed person must come to the same place that David came to in 1 Samuel 30:6. In the midst of dire circumstances and great distress he once again pulled himself out of the pit of despair.

David was greatly distressed, for the men spoke of stoning him because the souls of them all were bitterly grieved, each man for his sons and his daughters. But David encouraged and strengthened himself in the Lord his God. (Amplified Bible)

Notice the contrast in this verse. The men possessed by bitterness because of the loss of their families, could think of no other recourse than to turn their anger on David and stone him to death. David, however, having also lost his family, chose to rise up out of that bitterness and seek God.

As David strengthened and encouraged himself in the Lord, the guidance he needed for victory in the situation came. The guidance we need to get out of the pit will be available to us as well when we learn to strengthen ourselves in the Lord.

Looking up

David said in Psalm 61:2, *"From the end of the earth I will cry to You, when my heart is overwhelmed; lead me to the rock that is higher than I."*

When we feel ourselves shutting down in some area whether in a major or minor way, it is because we are looking at our circumstances only through human eyes. Have you ever noticed that you and I lack the ability to see past the end of our nose? How then do we come to the place where we think we know everything there is to know about a situation?

Moses looked up and began to see things through God's eyes, and when he did everything changed.

David had learned that when overwhelming feelings came to him, all he had to do was look up knowing that God would provide the answer he did not have within himself. He knew that God lives on a higher plane and He knows things and sees things that can only be revealed as we continue to look to Him.

At Marah the people were overwhelmed by their circumstances, but Moses looked up and began to see things through God's eyes, and when he did everything changed; the answer came and the people were able to make progress.

Maybe you are a person who has virtually lived your whole life feeling overwhelmed. If that is you, then today it is time to look up and see things from heaven's perspective.

The Effect of Walls in Our Life from the Past

As we have looked at the first definition for the name "Shur" we have learned that "walls" in our lives are a type of habitual response to the pressures we face, they are a type of defense mechanism, and basically a way of dealing with life we have learned as a result of hurts and wounds.

Walls will hinder our ability to believe God in certain areas. They will cause us to overreact to circumstances we find ourselves in, and they can cause us to shut down because of feeling overwhelmed by life. If you can identify with any of these areas, then acknowledging that truth can be the first step to freedom.

Let's now continue on to the next definition for the name "Shur."

SUMMARY: *From Overwhelmed to Overcoming*

Sometimes emotions linked to our past can be overblown; they can even cause us to shut down and avoid responsibilities that should be a part of normal life. The key to overcoming this temptation to quit, is learning how to encourage ourselves by looking at our circumstances through God's eyes.

Further Thought

1. What is it in your life that causes you to feel continually overwhelmed? Do you find yourself running away from or avoiding responsibility in that area?

2. Begin to practice strengthening yourself in the Lord. How do we do this? By availing ourselves of the sources of strength God has provided for us. For instance, the Bible tells us prayer can strengthen us (Colossians 1:9-11; Jude 20); being taught God's Word can strengthen us (Proverbs 24:5); leaning on Jesus can strengthen us (Philippians 4:13); and finally, praising and worshiping God can strengthen us (Psalm 8:2; Matthew 21:16).

3. In Psalm 61:2 David said when he was overwhelmed, he would look to God who could see things on a higher plane than he. In Isaiah 55:8-9 God declares, *"For My thoughts are not your thoughts, nor are your ways My ways,' says the Lord. 'For as the heavens are higher than the earth, so are My ways higher than your ways, and My thoughts than your thoughts."*

One time I was praying for one of my brothers because he was overwhelmed with so many responsibilities. Over and over I kept asking God to remove some of his load even though it consisted of legitimate things like job responsibilities and going to school in pursuit of a master's degree. One day as I was praying God impressed upon me that removing his load was not the only way He could answer prayer; He could just as easily give him more strength and grace to handle what he needed to do.

Many times when we feel overwhelmed God is saying, "This is not the time to draw back or quit, but instead it is time to pursue walking in more of my power and grace to overcome."

Can you begin today looking at the circumstance that always seems to overwhelm you in a new light? God sees things from a higher plane and as we look to Him, He is able to make us equal to the task for whatever we are facing.

CHAPTER NINE

Letting God be Our Fortress and Our Strength

I will say of the Lord, "He is my refuge and my fortress; my God, in Him will I trust." Psalm 91:2

The Wilderness of Shur holds a significant place in Old Testament Bible history. In Genesis 20:1 we are told Abraham dwelt there for a time. In Genesis 16:7 Hagar, Sarai's maidservant, had a visitation from the Angel of the Lord there, and then in Genesis 25:16-18 we are told that the descendents of Ishmael settled in this area.

We know the region of Shur included areas of fortification for the purpose of keeping Bedouin tribes out of the eastern border of Egypt. This is quite possibly the history behind the second definition for the name "Shur," which is a "fort" or a "fortified city."[20]

> *Unconsciously, the walls we have erected from our past become a type of false security.*

Let's look for a moment at the purpose of fortification. As we have seen in the example of Egypt, fortification is for the obvious purpose of self-protection and that is exactly what self-made walls from the past do in our lives. Unfortunately, this self-protection also produces self-imprisonment and constriction unlike God's supernatural walls that nurture and bring *real* protection.

Trusting in Our Own Walls for Protection

Unconsciously, the walls we have erected from our past become a type of false security. Hiding behind them and refusing to move forward is an effort to protect ourselves from further injury. Let's once again look at the example we see in the Israelites.

Before Israel began their God-ordained campaign to conquer the Promised Land, Moses put forth a series of blessings and cursings that would be poured out depending upon whether or not Israel would obey the voice of the Lord and carefully observe His commands.

As God's mouthpiece, Moses talked about this issue of "walls" in Deuteronomy 28:52:

They shall besiege you at all your gates until your high and fortified walls, in which you trust, come down throughout all your land; and they besiege you at all your gates throughout all your land which the Lord your God has given you.

This verse of warning would later prove to be prophetic because that is exactly what happened to Israel after many years of rebellion and repeated disobedience to God. At the time of Babylon's invasion into Judah, the Southern Kingdom of Israel, we are told in Jeremiah 39:8:

And the Chaldeans burned the king's house and the houses of the people with fire, and broke down the walls of Jerusalem.

This happened because Judah chose time and again to trust in her own defenses rather than letting God be her protector and defender.

The Downfall of Three Kings

In 2 Chronicles, Chapters Eleven through Sixteen, we read the story of three kings: *Rehoboam* the son of Solomon, his son *Abijah*, and finally his grandson, *Asa*. All three endeavored to fortify and build up the cities of Judah where Jerusalem was located, but over time in doing so, they quit trusting in God to preserve them which led to their downfall.

Sadly, even after seeing God do great miracles to deliver his grandfather, father, and himself from invasion of foreign nations, in 2 Chronicles 16:1-6 King Asa succumbs to fear and looks to his own ability to secure protection for Judah apart from God. In an act of panic, he gathers silver and gold from the treasuries of the house of the Lord to buy off the support of a neighboring king.

In the short run it looked as if the plan had succeeded and war had been avoided, but in verses 7-9 the prophet Hanani delivers a stinging word of rebuke from the Lord to him:

Because you have relied on the king of Syria, and have not relied on the Lord your God, therefore the army of the king of Syria has escaped from your hand. Were the Ethiopians and the Lubim not a huge army with very many chariots and horseman? Yet, because you relied on the Lord, He delivered them into your hand. For the eyes of the Lord run to and fro throughout the whole earth, to show Himself strong on behalf of those whose heart is loyal to Him. In this you have done foolishly; therefore from now on you shall have wars.

How many times have we relied on our own resources to deal with the difficulties of life rather than going to God about it? Are we quick to hide behind "walls" of anger, fear, resentment, manipulation, self-pity, addictions, and the like, yet slow to turn to God in time of stress and difficulty? When we use these types of self-defense against our circumstances, in the short term it may look like we have won, but make no mistake, we have done foolishly and instead of closing the door to future "wars" of difficulty, we have actually opened the door to more of the same.

When was the last time you experienced that "trigger" circumstance and instead of immediately responding in anger or with a sharp tongue, you closed your lips and went to God about it? James 4:2b expresses it this way: *"You fight and war. Yet you do not have because you do not ask."*

At the time of the incident at Marah, Israel had developed a "wall" of fear, self-pity, and complaining. Every time a difficulty came their way, they responded from this fortification; it was what they trusted in and all they could see. But God in His mercy, caused Moses to be a continual example before them, endeavoring to teach them how to trust in the Lord's protection and provision. Instead of complaining, Moses put his trust in God and cried out to Him for an answer.

How many times have we relied on our own resources to deal with the difficulties of life rather than going to God about it?

This is how God desires that we would live our lives. In Zechariah 2:4-5, Zechariah was given a vision of the restored Jerusalem:

Who said to him, "Run, speak to this young man, saying: 'Jerusalem shall be inhabited as towns without walls, because of the multitude of men and livestock in it. For I, says the Lord, 'will be a wall of fire all around her, and I will be the glory in her midst."

Let this be a lesson to us; if we do not learn to let God be our protector, defender and deliverer, we are destined to take all that responsibility upon ourselves. Thus, when we come to the realization that these self-made walls of protection do nothing but hinder us, our futile response is to continue fortifying and building, until in the end all we do is push ourselves farther away from people, farther away from God, and farther away from the new thing we really and truly desire in our lives.

King Asa's Epitaph

As we finish this line of thought, let's look at King Asa one more time. His final epitaph was that this had become a way of life for him. In 2 Chronicles 16:11-14 we are told that later in his reign he became severely diseased in his feet, but in his disease he did not seek the Lord for help, only the physicians. The implication here is that had he not succumbed to a diseased heart toward the Lord, this outward disease could have been taken care of.

What is the condition of our heart today? Are we loyal toward God? *This is a real key to bringing down the walls of our past: that we are quick to turn to God in all difficulty, allowing Him to become not only Lord over our circumstances but also Lord over our responses!*

LIVING LIFE FORWARD

SUMMARY: *Turning Our Defense Over to God*

When we continue to hide behind emotional walls two things will happen: these walls will increase and our trust in God will decrease. Holding on to an emotional wall will put us in a precarious situation because true security and protection from hurts and wounds can only come from God.

Further Thought

1. A number of years ago I went through a very difficult situation in which I suffered what I considered to be a painful injustice (I will comment on this further in Chapter Twelve). When I went to God about it, He let me know that the only way out was to let Him be my defender, meaning I would not be able to defend myself through verbal retaliation. Ouch! To that point I had never been able to keep my mouth closed in such a circumstance, but now I knew my victory would require it.

It took about ten months of seeking God before there was a turnaround, but when it happened it was complete. God moved in a big way to bring about my deliverance. Had I insisted on being my own defender, I may have had momentary satisfaction, but I believe the situation would have never been resolved. Make no mistake, God's defense may take longer, but in the end it will be worth it.

Do you have an area of your life where you need to switch defense attorneys? If you feel like you are getting nowhere in your case, it may be time to fire your "self-defense attorney" and allow God to become your defender.

2. During the time that I allowed God to be my defender, He began to talk to me about attitudes in my life that may have opened a door to the circumstance that happened to me. As I allowed Him to search my heart, walls of pride and offense were exposed. Up until that time, I had been blinded to the fact that they were there. Now I had to make a decision to let God do a cleansing work in me.

How did this cleansing work come about? I began to do an intensive personal study on what the Bible had to say about the areas of *humility* and *love*. As I endeavored to submit to what I was learning from God's Word, a change began to happen in me. By the time my deliverance came I was ready to forgive and to let go of resentment toward those who had hurt me, thus cutting ties to the past in this area.

While your "case" is in process, are you willing to allow God to shine His light on attitudes in your life that may have opened a door to the situation?

3. Ephesians 5:26b talks about *"the washing of water by the word."* What subject in God's Word do you need to begin to study to bring a cleansing into your life?

PART THREE

Beyond the Crisis

Chapter Ten

From Bondage to New Vision

Now we come to the third and final definition for the Wilderness of Shur and it is simply *"vision"* or *"to look around."* Let me put it to you this way: the Wilderness of Shur is not only the place where we become aware of and face up to the fact there are walls in our lives, and even walls that have become fortified cities, but it also is the place of vision, where God opens our eyes to see what we haven't seen before.

"Is this necessary?" you might ask. Absolutely, because a vital part of moving out of our past in order to live our lives forward is that we must discard the blinders of our past and allow God to give us a new vision for our future.

Hagar Needed a Vision for Her Future and So do We

In Genesis 16 we find the story of Hagar's encounter with the Wilderness of Shur. Hagar was an Egyptian maidservant who belonged to Abram (Abraham) and Sarai (Sarah). In verse sixteen we read that she fled to the Wilderness of Shur to escape mistreatment from Sarai. What a vivid picture this is of someone running from the source of their pain.

The first thing we learn from Hagar's experience is that God is always there waiting for us.

Look at verses 7-10:

Now the Angel of the Lord found her by a spring of water in the wilderness, by the spring on the way to Shur. And He said, "Hagar, Sarai's maid, where have you come from, and where are you going?" She said, "I am fleeing from the presence of my mistress Sarai." The Angel of the Lord said to her, "Return to your mistress, and submit yourself under her hand." Then the Angel of the Lord said to her, "I will multiply your descendents exceedingly, so that they shall not be counted for multitude."

First, it is to be noted that Hagar is addressed as *"Sarai's maid,"* and it becomes quickly apparent that the Angel knows who she is and who she belongs to. Yet He asks, *"Where have you come from?"* Is this because Hagar needed to be reminded?

The Angel's question is reminiscent of the divine question to Adam and Eve after the fall: *"Where are you?"* (Genesis 3:9) And the similar question to Elijah after he ran in fear from Jezebel: *"What are you doing here, Elijah?"* (1 Kings 19:9). In both instances we see people who were in the wrong place and headed in the wrong direction. God was endeavoring to draw them out of hiding and back to Himself.

The fact that Hagar was *"on the way to Shur"* indicates she was intent on returning to Egypt; she was headed in the wrong direction. Hagar needed a redirection back to God and back to His purpose for her.

Next came the question: *"Where are you going?"* Notice that Hagar answered the first question, but not the second because the second had to do with her future. Hagar was about to find out that the God who knew and cared about her past was also the God who held her future in His hand.

> ***Hagar needed a redirection back to God and back to His purpose for her.***

My husband and I minister weekly at a nearby county jail. One evening I had just finished speaking when a young lady approached me for prayer. Wiping tears from her eyes she looked at me and said, "I am so afraid that I don't have a future because there has been so much hurt in my past. So many bad things have happened."

As I prayed for her the Lord impressed upon me that she could be confident of her future because God held it in His hands. The same was true for Hagar. She may have received a vision of the Lord at this spring of water, but she also needed a vision for her future. She needed the bitter waters of her life to be turned sweet, but how could this happen?

God's Vision Gives Hope

Finally, Hagar is instructed by the Angel of the Lord to return and face the problem that brought her here rather than fleeing from it. But, notice, even though she must return, having met face-to-face with the Lord, she now does so with new knowledge, understanding, and hope. God has seen, He has heard, and He has answered.

Here is the amazing thing: The Angel went on to tell her that if she would obey, He would multiply her descendents so greatly they could not be numbered! We are to understand that blessing would come upon her life as a result of facing up to and dealing with the source of her pain.

We must ask ourselves the same question, "Where have we come from, and where are we going?" Do we need a redirection in our lives? Could it be that we have been running from or avoiding relationships, intimacy with people or God, responsibilities, doing the right thing, or any number of other difficult areas because we know if we head in that direction we will have to face the pain? In our thinking, sheer avoidance is easier than the pain.

But God says to you and me today, "Return and be healed knowing that I will be with you." And as we are obedient to His voice, blessing will come upon our lives. In Jeremiah 30:17a the Lord speaks to Israel and to you and me:

> "'For I will restore health to you and heal you of your wounds,' says the Lord."

Before leaving, Hagar named the place *Beer Lahai Roi* meaning, "*Well of the One Who lives and Sees me.*" Not only did God *see* Hagar, but just like Moses, He also caused her to see what she had not seen before. When Hagar was obedient to throw this new-found hope into her bitter waters, they were made sweet. Hagar was on her way to healing.

SUMMARY: *A Vision of Hope for Our Future*

Only God can open our eyes to see the truth in our lives and in our situations. This is not always easy, but essential. When we embrace God's truth, we will find that it always has a vision of hope attached to it.

Further Thought

1. In the Bible, Egypt is a type of the world and what it has to offer. Just like Hagar, many people have headed back to "Egypt" when things seemingly became too difficult. Egypt was not the answer for Hagar and it is not the answer for us. Thankfully, God intercepted Hagar halfway there, turned her attention back to Him, and began a healing work in her heart.

In the midst of your difficulty have you found yourself being tempted to return to "Egypt"? Has God been speaking to your heart in an effort to turn your attention back to Him?

2. Like the young lady at the jail, do you feel your life is too full of bondage to have any hope for your future? Again, in Jeremiah 29:11 God says, *"For I know the thoughts that I think toward you, says the Lord, thoughts of peace and not*

evil, to give you a future and a hope." Would it interest you to know that this verse was written to people in captivity as a result of great bondage in their lives? But right in the middle of their bondage God was declaring that He still had a future for them if they would just turn and begin to seek Him with all their heart.

Are you ready to turn today to begin seeking God with all your heart? The moment you do, He is waiting to fill you with His hope and give you a fresh vision for your future.

3. How important is a vision for our future? Proverbs 29:18a (KJV) says, *"Where there is no vision, the people perish."* Hagar and her unborn son may have perished had she not met up with and responded to the Angel of the Lord. Hagar was headed down a dead-end road, but a fresh vision turned her in a direction of blessing.

When God asks the question, *"Where are you going?"* it is time to look to Him for the answer.

4. Do you feel like God has forgotten you? Hagar certainly did, but her encounter with God proved to her that was not the case. Make no mistake; we serve the God "Who sees."

Several times in this book we have we have discussed the woman who was made straight in Luke 13. Eighteen years crippled had most certainly affected her self-esteem and probably her social interactions. I can picture her attending church Sunday after Sunday thinking no one noticed her, no one cared; but Jesus saw her and called her to Himself.

Do you feel you have been "crippled" in some area of your life? Do you feel no one sees or cares? Be encouraged because "The One who lives and sees" takes notice of you and He will raise you up.

Chapter Eleven

Embracing Our Future

You and I have the advantage of hindsight as we read the biblical account of the challenge at Marah. From this vantage point we understand that once the answer from God had come, it was time for the people to start moving forward into the future He had for them. Verse 27 concludes Exodus Fifteen with this:

> *Then they came to Elim, where there were twelve wells of water and seventy palm trees; so they camped there by the waters.*

We will look further at the significance of Elim in Chapter Fourteen, but for now let us understand that Elim was a place of blessing and refreshing. The tragedy, however, is that most people never get to go to *Elim*, at least not permanently, because they do what the Israelites did at Marah: *they give in to their flesh - their undisciplined human nature - and complain.*

Have you ever been on the *other side* of a challenge, and realized God really *did* have a plan, He *was* faithful after all, and He *did* bring you through and suddenly you felt rather sheepish about all the ranting and raving? At least I hope that is the case! I have been there more times than I would like to admit. We know we are beginning to mature in the things of God when we can avoid all of that and believe in the faithfulness of God on *this side* of the challenge.

Do You Need a "Moses" in Your Life?

Moses was the saving grace for the people of Israel as they faced the challenge at Marah. Personally I am grateful for the "Moses'" God has put in my life; people who knew what to do when I didn't. If we are smart, we will recognize these people and follow their lead. Here is a lightning-fast clue: When you find yourself frustrated, complaining, or even ranting and raving, quickly understand you have obviously lost sight of the right thing to do. At that point the best course of action is to find someone who does know what to do in God and hook up with them. This means observing them, listening to them, and running with them, until you can get back on track.

This is exactly the situation in which Naomi found herself as described in the book of Ruth. She and her husband, who had been residents of Bethlehem, made a decision to move their family to Moab in the midst of famine. To be sure, they were facing a crisis, but they compounded it by making a bad decision in response. It was certainly not an act of faith on their part. Instead of trusting in God to be their provider in the land He had called them to, they moved to the land of an enemy nation seeking sustenance there.

How many times have we made bad, faithless choices in life and then later blamed God for difficulties we faced as a result of those choices?

Over a period of ten years in Moab, Naomi gained two daughters-in-law, but also experienced the death of her husband and both of her sons. Upon hearing there was now food in Bethlehem, she returned with one of her daughters-in-law, Ruth. In Ruth 1:19-21 we find Naomi's state of mind as she entered the city.

Now the two of them went until they came to Bethlehem. And it happened, when they had come to Bethlehem, that all the city was excited because of them; and the women said, "Is this Naomi?" But she said to them, "Do not call me Naomi (Pleasant); call me Mara (Bitter), for the Almighty has dealt very bitterly with me. I went out full, and the Lord has brought me home again empty. Why do you call me Naomi, since the Lord has testified against me, and the Almighty has afflicted me?"

How many times have we made bad, faithless choices in life and later blamed God for difficulties we faced as a result of those choices? Naomi definitely overreacted in her accusations against God. She may have come home to Bethlehem, but she did not come empty-handed; she most certainly had brought her past with her.

In Ruth, Naomi's daughter-in-law, we see this must not always be the case. Ruth also had a potentially painful past.

She had lost her husband, she had no children, and she had grown up in a culture completely hostile toward God. But over and over again she displayed by her attitude of faith that she had chosen to leave her past in Moab and to embrace her new future in God, which would include a husband, a son, and a place in the lineage of Jesus Christ.

To begin with, Ruth was a person who was ready to change, unlike her sister-in-law who chose to stay to stay in Moab (interestingly enough, we never hear of this sister-in-law again). What made Ruth's decision successful was that her change was rooted in her trust in God (Ruth 1:13-17). Once she made the change, she continued to obediently look to God for guidance and provision in every circumstance she faced. Not once do we hear her complain.

We mentioned earlier that the Wilderness of Shur, which is where Marah was located, is also the place where God opens our eyes to see what we have not seen before. Naomi needed to have her eyes opened to see the truth of her situation. Just like God had been waiting to minister healing to Hagar, He was also waiting to minister healing to Naomi. Naomi needed a "Moses" and she found it in Ruth. Little-by-little as she observed Ruth humbly reaching out to God in faith for daily provision, Naomi's spiritual sight was restored, and she got back on track with God's purpose for her life.

Just the other day I was suffering physically from a cold; nevertheless, I had pushed on to accomplish what I needed to do by that evening. Late in the afternoon, I was feeling pretty drained and it seemed that everything I touched turned into a hassle. I know you have been there! Before I knew it, frustration had set in and my emotions took control. I had allowed my tiredness to turn into upset and self-pity. As embarrassing as it was, I tottered on the verge of tears, until "Moses," my husband Chuck, offered his perspective.

"Remember so-and-so who we recently visited in the hospital and be glad that is not you tonight," he said, and how right he was. As is usually the case in these things, God had already been speaking the exact same correction to my heart, but it took Chuck to really drive it home to my mind and emotions. I immediately straightened up and began to give thanks to God for how good He had been to me.

Naomi was not the only person in the Bible who needed her spiritual sight restored to see God's goodness once again. The apostle Paul had also been delivered out of a bitter past. He described it this way in Philippians 3:13-14:

Brethren, I do not count myself to have apprehended; but one thing I do, <u>forgetting those things which are behind and reaching forward to those things which are ahead</u>, I press toward the goal for the prize of the upward call of God in Christ Jesus.

Living Our Lives Forward

As we have already seen, the big difference between Naomi and Ruth is that one was embracing her past while the other was embracing her future. The lesson we learn from Ruth's life is that because, by faith, she had cut ties with the cursing of her past, she was now free to step into the blessing of her future in God.

<u>How do we cut ties with the hurts and wounds of our past?</u> Actually, it happens on two levels:

1. Daily
2. In degrees over time

<u>On a daily basis we must decide to trust and obey God</u> in the present regardless of what has happened in the past. A very important principle in God is that we are to live our lives

"forward" in Him. Again the apostle Paul said, *"Pressing, reaching forward to those things which are ahead"* and in Exodus 14:15 we hear God's instruction to *"Go forward"* as the Israelites looked at the Red Sea with feelings of panic overwhelming them.

You must understand that you cannot cross the Red Sea in front of you if you are standing still or continually taking steps backward; no, you must *daily* make a decision to go forward. It may not always be easy and it will take faith, but as you are persistent to daily walk in this direction, you will eventually find yourself on the other side of the sea with your enemies drowned behind you. As Deuteronomy 7:22 told us, your complete deliverance may come little-by-little and in degrees over time, but *it will come.*

Putting on the New Man

The Red Sea crossing was a type (or a picture) of our death, burial, and resurrection in Christ. When we receive Jesus as our Lord and Savior, we cross over to new life in Him. Second Corinthians 5:17 says, *"Therefore, if anyone is in Christ, he is a new creation; old things have passed away; behold, all things have become new."*

The book of Colossians actually calls us a "New Man" in Christ. In Colossians 3:9-10 we are told, *"Do not lie to one another, since you have put off the old man with his deeds, and have put on the new man who is renewed in knowledge according to the image of Him who created him."*

Too many of us are still dragging around the old "dead man" of our past.

This is talking about someone who has been born again and has become a "new man" in Christ and yet they continue to allow their "old man" to dictate how they will react and respond to situations in the present. We see this in the example of Naomi. She was a believer, but she was allowing the "old man" of her past to control her present.

Colossians says that knowledge is the key that will keep us from living in the past and enable us to put on the new man of our future in Christ. What knowledge would this be? The knowledge of what the Bible says about the areas of our life where we have been wounded and how Jesus, out of His great love for us, paid the price to heal us, deliver us, and set us free. As we progressively grow in this knowledge, we become more and more free.

Too many of us are still dragging around the old, "dead man" of our past. Again, we must *"clear out the old to make room for the new."* Ruth did this as she set her face for Bethlehem and made this solemn commitment to Naomi in Ruth 1:16b-17, *"...For wherever you go, I will go; and wherever you lodge, I will lodge; your people shall be my people, and your God, my God. Where you die, I will die, and there will I be buried. The Lord do so to me, and more also, if anything but death parts you and me."*

Yes, Ruth was a "Moses" to Naomi because she was a person who chose to live her life forward in God. Did God have a new thing on the horizon for Ruth? He most certainly did, and Ruth was able to embrace it because she had cut ties with the hurts of her past. Not only did she marry the most eligible bachelor in Bethlehem, but she also gave birth to a son who would become the grandfather of King David and a member of the ancestry of Jesus Christ.

SUMMARY: *Moving Forward into Our Future*

Regardless of past mistakes, moving forward into our future will require a decision to no longer allow our past to dictate how we will react and respond in the present. Success will come from growth in the knowledge of God's Word, but God may also strategically place someone in our life to be an example that we can learn from and follow.

Further Thought

1. Have you struggled with resentment toward God because of difficulties in your life? Is it possible that bad, faithless choices were to blame rather than Him? One day I was praying for someone who was struggling with resentment toward God. As I prayed the Lord caused me to see that the real resentment this person had was not toward God, but toward himself because of mistakes made in the past.

Is it possible the resentment you feel toward God is really resentment toward yourself? The beginning of your future may be your willingness to not only forgive God, but to also forgive yourself.

2. Do you need your spiritual sight restored? Is there a "Moses" that God has placed in your life? If discouragement has caused you to lose your spiritual focus, begin to look around you for that person God has put in your path to be the example you need.

Sometimes it can even be the other way around: the person God has put in your path may be the catalyst for showing you your spiritual sight is in need of restoration. Years ago this very thing happened to me. During a period of six months, I had allowed myself to grow "cold" to the things of God. One day my cousin came to visit and she was "hot" for the things of God. Her joy and excitement rubbed me the wrong way, but at the same time it was also a wake-up call to let me know something needed to change in my life.

Has someone recently been a wake-up call in your life? If so, respond to that call; I am so glad I did!

3. Have you made a decision to *"put off the old man"* and to instead *"put on the new man"* you have become in Christ? Ephesians 4:23 says we do this by being *"renewed in the spirit of our mind."* This means we no longer respond to difficulties as we once did, but instead respond from the wisdom of God's Word as we daily spend time in it. As we

feed upon God's Word our thinking begins to change which, in turn, leads to a change in our actions and responses.

Do you have a plan for putting God's Word in you on a daily basis?

Chapter Twelve

Choosing to See

If we take a closer look at Moses, we will discover he was a man who not only knew what to do, but also chose to do it. This is very important. We mentioned earlier that a big part of Israel's problem was getting beyond the bondage they had encountered in their past. Having said that, let us not forget that like Israel, Naomi, and Ruth, Moses also had "a past." In fact he had experienced so much failure and disappointment in that past that it was forty years before God could begin to speak to him and deal with him about his calling to deliver Israel.

When God appeared to Moses through a burning bush, it was on the backside of the desert (Exodus 3:1). Moses had made his home there after running away from his disappointments and failures many years before. Have we learned yet that we can run away from people and places, but we cannot run away from God?

As God re-established His call on Moses' life, Moses had to make a decision to leave his place of hiding and to begin, by faith, living his life forward in God. Each time Israel rebelled against the authority God had given Moses, he had an opportunity and a temptation to return to his place of hiding.

When we compare Moses to the children of Israel, I believe we can understand that a big part of living our lives forward simply has to do with our choices. Are we going to take God at His Word and obey Him or not? Moses made a choice that day at Marah; instead of returning to the backside of the desert, he cried out to God and when he did, God opened his eyes to see a tree. Not only did he see the tree, God also caused him to understand that if he threw it into the waters, something would change.

This tree had to have been there all along, but Moses had not seen it, or at least not the significance of it, until God opened his eyes. Here again we see the choice Moses made. As he went before God he had to be willing to see and accept what he had not seen before, and then to be obedient to throw that into the situation.

> *A big part of living our lives forward simply has to do with our choices.*

The application to you and me is obvious. In our struggles are we willing to make the choice to cry out to God instead of giving in to our ongoing emotional issues? Are we willing to accept that God could show us something about our past or about our circumstances we have not seen before? And finally, are we willing to take what He shows us and throw it into our situation?

Many people question *God's* willingness to help in their time of need; however, the real problem is that they are asking the wrong question. God's willingness to help us has been firmly established in His Word. We have already seen that God has displayed His willingness through the many miracles He has performed, but we can also consider Matthew 8:1-4. There we find that when the leper came and asked if Jesus was willing to heal him, Jesus' compassionate answer was, "*I am willing; be cleansed.*" The real question is not whether or not God is willing, but rather, *are we willing to follow through on what He shows us?*

Focusing Our Attention Forward

In order to have a willing heart toward God, we must first have a heart focused in His direction. This focus will create the spiritual hunger needed for willingness.

We have a very nice walking path right behind our house. This walking path winds around our neighborhood, which is a significantly large housing addition. I have been walking on this track for several years now, but just the other day, as I was doing my morning jaunt, I noticed an unusual looking tree in someone's backyard I had not noticed before. I was immediately struck with the question, "How could I have missed this?" After all, I had walked by this tree many, many times and it wasn't like it was just hidden or blended in with all the other trees. No, this tree stood alone and it was markedly different than any other tree I remembered seeing. I literally had no idea what type of tree it was!

How could this happen? Simple, I had not been paying attention. The same thing can happen in our spiritual lives. Many times God has already put a "tree," an obvious answer in our path, but because we are not focused in - we are not paying attention - we miss it. It is not that God hasn't already provided answers; it's that we haven't seen them.

God's answer to our challenges will always head us in a forward direction.

When Moses fell on his face and cried out to God, he clearly demonstrated he was paying attention and his heart was willing. When I was a younger Christian I thought everyone around me could hear from God except me and I wondered what the problem was. As I began to mature a little spiritually, I gradually gained an understanding that the problem was *me*. The other people around me were paying attention, but I wasn't. As a result, they were displaying a spiritual hunger I didn't have.

What do I mean by "paying attention"? Proverbs 3:6 puts it this way, *"In all your ways acknowledge Him, and He shall direct your paths."* Throughout our day, in all that we do, we need to purposely have an ear open to God. Paying attention means we expect God to speak to us, to direct us, and to show us what we need to see. When we read His Word, we expect Him to speak to us through it; when we pray, we expect God to answer us; and when we worship, we have an ear open to hear what He will minister back to us.

God's answer to our challenges will always head us in a forward direction; therefore, if our focus is still on our past, we could very well miss what He is trying to show us.

Developing Spiritual Discernment

The ability to pay *spiritual* attention can and must be developed. In Matthew 16:1-4 Jesus chided the Pharisees and Sadducees because they had well-developed natural discernment that allowed them to anticipate weather patterns, but they had failed to develop spiritual discernment that would enable them to recognize the signs of the time or, in other words, spiritual things.

Listen to what the Apostle Paul said about spiritual hearing and seeing in Acts 28:26-27 as he quoted the Prophet Isaiah:

Go to this people and say: "Hearing you will hear, and shall not understand; and seeing you will see, and not perceive; for the hearts of this people have grown dull. Their ears are hard of hearing, and their eyes they have closed, lest they should see with their eyes and hear with their ears, lest they should understand with their hearts and turn, so that I should heal them."

Do you see what happened to the Israelites at the bitter waters of Marah? Instead of acknowledging God in the midst of their difficulty, they showed they were hard-of-hearing and had closed their eyes; therefore, the understanding they needed could not come, and without understanding they couldn't turn - change - and without turning, they would forsake the healing God had for them.

How does a person become spiritually hard-of-hearing or spiritually blind? It is the end result of not paying attention. When we are complaining, we are not paying attention. In that moment the only thing we are paying attention to is ourselves; that is serious because as long as we are focused on ourselves, we are not focused on God; thus, we will be hindered from hearing Him. We could also go on and say that when we are depressed, discouraged, or yielding to self-pity, fear, or worry, we are not paying attention.

Let's take this a step further and say as long as we are angry or harboring unforgiveness or resentment, we are not paying attention. In this instance, we may be putting all our attention and focus on another person, and as long as we are doing so, we are again, not able to hear from God.

Maybe you were hurt in the past, and the reason that hurt seems to keep coming up to revisit you is because you are still blaming the other person like the Israelites blamed Moses. There certainly may have been injustice in what you experienced, but what about your part in this? We must come to the realization that we can't do anything about the other person, but we can do something about ourselves; we can turn our focus back on God and begin to pay attention.

What is the Tree You Need to See?

What kind of tree has God put in your *walking path* to see regarding your past? Is it the tree of forgiving someone, or humbling yourself in some way, or the tree of rising up in faith instead of continually cowering in fear?

I am convinced it is usually something we are not aware of in our lives. We can actually have spiritual "blind spots" where we *think* we *know* something from God's Word, but are oblivious to the fact that *we are not doing it.*

Consider the following possible "trees" God could open our eyes to:

- Choosing to walk in love instead of giving in to jealousy or offense
- Choosing to trust God instead of fearing man
- Choosing to finally forgive yourself
- Choosing to praise God in your "wilderness" instead of giving in to discouragement and depression
- Choosing to cast your care and to walk in God's peace
- *choosing to release myself from my past*
- *choosing to resist the stronghold of the past*

I went through one particularly difficult circumstance in which God made it clear to me that my tree of obedience was to keep a guard on my mouth. The only time I could talk about the issue was to either speak what His Word had to say about it or to give Him praise that He was working in my behalf.

God's instruction was a very hard thing for me to do at the time, but I had to make a decision: *Did I want my bitter waters turned sweet or not? Did I want this cursing in my life turned into blessing or not?* Bottom line, you cannot be half-hearted and expect your walls to come down. We must decide to obey God and stick to it.

Much of time we must come to the realization that we can't do anything about the other person, but we can do something about ourselves.

Every difficulty we encounter will have a "tree." We will make great strides toward healing of past hurts and wounds when we forget about the other people involved and begin asking God to show us *our tree* in the situation. Blaming others will keep us in a state of blindness. As much as we may not want to see it in our flesh, we must understand it was the "tree" that turned the bitter waters sweet.

In that particular difficulty, along with watching the words of my mouth, I did a lot of praying and seeking God. There was no doubt I had suffered an injustice; in fact, one of the worst I ever had, but through this time of seeking God began to show me areas of weakness in my life that had worsened the situation. As I submitted these areas to Him, I came into newfound spiritual vision and depth of relationship with God that brought great healing into my heart and a new outlook for my future.

The Tree that Bore Our Cursing

Finally, we cannot conclude a look at this "tree" without expressing the fact that it also represents the cross of Jesus Christ. Paul teaches us in Galatians 3:13-14 that Jesus took upon Himself our cursing and our bitterness, so we could receive the blessing and become "sweet" in Him:

Christ has redeemed us from the curse of the law, having become a curse for us (for it is written, "Cursed is everyone who hangs on a tree"), that the blessing of Abraham might come upon the Gentiles in Christ Jesus, that we might receive the promise of the Spirit through faith.

The most vital thing we can understand in this study is Jesus bore our cursing - our bitterness, our sin, our fear, our anger, our hurt, our failure - and He nailed it to the cross. He paid the price for our freedom in His own body and then arose to the right hand of the Father to guarantee our deliverance. Hebrews 7:25 tells us He now *"always lives to make intercession for them"*.

Hebrews 4:14-16 gives us clear instruction for the temptations we face:

> *Seeing then that we have a great High Priest who has passed through the heavens, Jesus the Son of God, let us hold fast our confession. For we do not have a High Priest who cannot sympathize with our weaknesses, but was in all points tempted as we are, yet without sin. Let us therefore come boldly to the throne of grace, that we may obtain mercy and find grace to help in time of need.*

Because Jesus has walked where we walk, He understands our weaknesses and the temptations we face. Out of this understanding He has provided all of the grace and mercy we will need to overcome if we will boldly come before Him to ask.

This mercy and grace has always been available. The Old Testament saints looked in faith toward the cross of Jesus and His sacrifice and found salvation, provision, and deliverance. You and I now look back in faith on what Jesus did and receive salvation, provision, and deliverance from whatever bondage we have experienced.

My prayer for you today is that you have eyes to see what Jesus did on your behalf and a willing heart to obey what He shows you to do.

SUMMARY: *The Tree that Turns the Bitterness Sweet*

Our choice is the catalyst for a hope-filled future in God. We must choose to cry out to God for help in the midst of our circumstances, and once again choose to see and obey what He shows us. God has already provided a "tree" of deliverance for every situation we face.

Further Thought

1. One of the primary ways God will speak to us is through His Word. For this reason it is especially important for us to read and study His Word on a daily basis. Each time we open the Word of God, we are in essence saying, "God I am paying attention and I am giving You opportunity to speak to me today."

I have lost count of how many times God has given me direction for that day as I read His Word in the morning. Even before I knew what the day would bring, I already had the guidance I needed. This came about simply by giving Him opportunity.

Are you daily giving God opportunity to speak needed direction into your life? Do you listen for His voice with an expectant ear?

2. What causes a person to be willing to see the "tree" that needs to be thrown into their difficulty? In my situation, I finally hurt badly enough in the present circumstance that I was willing to do something about the bondages that had emerged from my past. Unfortunately, too many times this is the case with most people.

The best scenario is to keep an ongoing humble heart before God so He can deal with us before our circumstances become dire. In years since, I have learned not to fear God's working in my life. Once you get a taste of the freedom it brings, you will welcome His healing touch with open arms.

Even if you are not in a dire situation today, can you ask God to do a preventative work in your heart?

3. Hebrews 4:16 declares Jesus paid the price for God's mercy and grace to be extended to us. How does this affect the bondages we deal with? We could view God's mercy as His compassion and forgiveness for our past sins, and His grace as divine strengthening to help us in our present and

future time of need. No matter which direction we look in our lives, God has already provided.

Will you come boldly before His throne of grace today and ask for the mercy and grace you need?

CHAPTER THIRTEEN

Jehovah Rapha, The Lord Our Healer

As we are about to see with the Israelites at Marah, God knew they needed more than just the healing of their present circumstances; they also needed healing within if they were going to live their lives forward in His plan and purpose for them. God was making this healing available, but the realization of it would require a new revelation.

In the Old Testament, one way God revealed His character and nature to Israel and to us was through divine names and titles He ascribed to Himself. Essential aspects of covenant relationship between God and His people were also expressed in these names. God would pick key moments of difficulty and distress to introduce each of these titles and Exodus 15 gives us one such very important incident.

After the bitter waters were turned sweet supernaturally by the power of God, verses 25 and 26 announce, *"...There He made a statute and an ordinance for them, and there He tested them, and said, 'If you diligently heed the voice of the Lord your God and do what is right in His sight, give ear to His commandments and keep all His statutes, I will put none of these diseases on you which I have brought on the Egyptians. For I am the Lord who heals you."*

The word for *heal* in this verse means *"to cure, to repair, to mend, or to restore health."*[21] Herbert Lockyer provides this definition: *"The word 'heal' means 'to mend' as a garment is mended, 'to repair' as a building is reconstructed, and 'to cure' as a diseased person is restored to health."*[22] The root of the Hebrew word for *"heal"* is translated as *physician* in Jeremiah 8:22:

Is there no balm in Gilead, is there no physician there? Why then is there no recovery for the health of the daughter of my people?

Because the nation of Israel had not heeded or obeyed the voice of the Lord their God, they found themselves in a place of great distress.

J.A. Thompson explains it this way:

> *For the wounds of the people's flesh there was relief in the soothing balsam of Gilead or from the attentive care of a doctor. Gilead on the eastern side of the Jordan River was famous already in patriarchal times for its healing balsams. The "balm of Gilead" was evidently one such healing substance. On the physical level there was healing to be found. But Gilead's balm and the doctor's care would not suffice for the deep wound inflicted on Jeremiah's own people. There could be no regeneration of Judah's health when her spirit remained rebellious and unregenerate.* [23]

The Great Physician

Jesus is our Great Physician. He is revealed as Jehovah Rapha in Exodus 15:26, *"the Lord who heals you."* He is the

One who mends, repairs, cures and brings restoration into our lives. Through the revelation of the Holy Spirit, Jeremiah understood that the real need of the people was healing on a spiritual level, healing that would bring a change of heart on the inside. Their wound went much deeper than any physical symptoms they were experiencing. If the people only pursued natural medicines and treatments, their restoration would be temporary and superficial in nature. Their only hope for lasting wholeness would be found in the healing touch of the Great Physician, Jehovah Rapha.

No matter how impossible your situation seems, it is not incurable or too severe for the healing power of God.

Much like many people today, Israel had laid aside the presence and the commandments of Jehovah Rapha and had pursued natural remedies for their illnesses and wounds. Like the self-erected walls we discussed earlier, in the end, all these remedies failed them. Look at Jeremiah 30:12-14a:

For thus says the Lord: "Your affliction is incurable, your wound is severe. There is no one to plead your *cause, that you may be bound up; you have no healing medicines. All your lovers have forgotten you..."*

The day we finally realize our only hope for real healing and restoration is in God, is the day things can begin to turn around in our lives. No matter how impossible your situation seems, it is not incurable or too severe for the healing power of God.

Here we see that while these people were still sick and wounded, God was declaring He had a plan for their deliverance. Listen to the promise of verse 17:

"For I will restore health to you, and heal you of your wounds," says the Lord...

Again, the Hebrew word for *heal* used in the above verse is the same word *"rapha"* we have been examining from Exodus 15:26. Over and over we see this word used in connection to physical healing and inward restoration.

Psalm 103:2-3 declares:

> *Bless the Lord, O my soul, and forget not all His benefits: Who forgives all your iniquities, who heals all your diseases.*

As already discussed in Chapter Twelve, Isaiah 53:4-5 reveals that the reason Jesus can heal us of inward hurts, sorrows, and wounds while simultaneously healing our physical bodies is because He carried all of these upon Himself and paid the ultimate price for that inward and outward healing:

> *Surely He has borne our griefs (sicknesses) and carried our sorrows (pains); yet we esteemed Him stricken, smitten by God, and afflicted. But He was wounded for our transgressions, He was bruised for our iniquities; the chastisement for our peace was upon Him, and by His stripes we are healed.*

Consider also Psalm 147:3 which says, "He *heals the broken hearted and binds up their wounds.*"

The Hebrew word translated *wound* in this verse, comes from a root referring to physical pain as well as to emotional sorrow.[24]

Finally, it is very interesting that this same word, *rapha*, is used in the verse we looked at previously in 2 Kings 2:22:

So the water remains healed to this day, according to the word of Elisha which he spoke.

Healed Inside and Out

Is it becoming clear that we serve the God who desires to heal and remove the cursing from our past so we are free to live our lives forward? But having looked at these verses, we now must go back to Exodus 15:26 because this is the place and the circumstance in which God chose to first reveal Himself as Healer. Why would this be so important to note? Again, Herbert Lockyer gives us insight:

In any phase of Bible study we may undertake, it is important to bear in mind what Dr. A.T. Pierson calls, The Law of First Mention. It will be found that so often, the first mention of a person, or place, or a doctrine, or word, is an embryo of a feature or a fact for which there is fuller development. [25]

Hence, the first mention of a particular word, or in this case a divine title for God, many times will give us fundamental understanding of it's meaning for our lives.

The crisis at Marah teaches us that the physical healing we seek may need to begin with emotional or spiritual healing.

To begin with you might wonder, "Why would God give a promise concerning healing in the midst of an incident involving emotional and spiritual issues being exposed and dealt with?" And then we might wonder why God would choose to use this same word *rapha* in context of the water being purified in 2 Kings 2:22, which we saw to be a type of purifying in our lives.

But having looked at all the previous scripture references, it becomes clear that much of the time there is a big connection between what happens to us emotionally or spiritually and what happens to us physically, whether that be in our bodies or in our circumstances. Therefore, the crisis at Marah teaches us that the physical healing we seek may need to begin with emotional or spiritual healing.

In the New Testament we also see this same connection. A portion of Isaiah 53:5 is quoted in 1 Peter 2:24:

Who Himself bore our sins in His own body on the tree, that we, having died to sins, might live for righteousness – by whose stripes you were healed.

Verses 18 through 24 of 1 Peter Chapter Two begin by talking about emotional issues such as people treating you unfairly and suffering because of doing right, and finishes with the above classic verse used so many times in prayer for physical healing.

Whether we look at the Old or New Testament, the good news is Jesus wants to heal us spiritually, emotionally, and physically and He has made covenant provision for that. The very fact that one of His revealed names is Jehovah Rapha, tells us that healing, restoration, and wholeness are actually a part of His very nature.

Wholeness for Naaman

In 2 Kings 5 we read the account of Naaman, the leper, commander of the Syrian army. Naaman traveled a long way to seek healing through the prophet Elisha, but little did he know God had much more than physical healing planned for him. It took a decision to obey, and humility on his part, but in the end Naaman walked away whole. God not only healed his leprosy, but also his heart. Naaman returned to his country a new man inside and out.

This is what God longs to do for you and me if only we will choose to obey and humble ourselves before Him. We can be healed inside and out when we embrace the presence of Jehovah Rapha.

SUMMARY: *A New Vision is Not Enough; We Also Need a New Revelation*

In the midst of their difficulty, Israel received a new revelation of God as they came to know Him by His covenant name of Jehovah Rapha. We need the same revelation today. A study of this divine name teaches us that the outward healing we seek may need to begin with emotional or spiritual healing.

Further Thought

1. In 2 Kings 20:1-11, King Hezekiah is sick and at the point of death. The prophet Isaiah announces to him that he should put his house in order because he will not live. How many people have received such a report only to accept it as inevitable? I once spoke with someone whose brother was told by a doctor he would not survive the cancer attacking his body. The brother's response was, "Well, I guess that's it. I am going to die."

This was not the case with Hezekiah. Upon hearing his report, verse 2 says he turned his face to the wall and prayed to God. Verse 3 goes on to say he *"wept bitterly."* Just as we saw earlier in the case of Hannah, this man took the bitterness of his heart and turned it into an impassioned prayer to the Great Physician. Immediately, the prophet Isaiah returned with a response from God: "*I have heard your prayer, I have seen your tears; surely I will heal* (rapha) *you*" (verse 5). Later Hezekiah received successful medical treatment, but the real turning point was his initial prayer to God.

Have you resigned yourself to the fact that your situation in "terminal"? Are you instead willing to take the bitterness of your heart and turn it into an impassioned prayer to God? If so, just like Hezekiah, today can be a turning point in your life.

2. Like the people of Israel in the book of Jeremiah, the woman with the issue of blood (Mark 5:21-34) had spent all she had on natural physicians, but in the end only grew worse. This was obviously a determined and desperate woman in the pursuit of her healing; but it was not until the day she took natural determination and turned it into spiritual determination that she was made healed and whole.

Is it time to take all the energy and passion you have expended in search of natural healing for the circumstances you face, and turn it into a determined pursuit of the healing and wholeness that can only come from God?

3. Do you need more than just physical healing in your life? Have you considered that wholeness comes when we allow God to heal us inside and out?

In 2 Kings 5, Namaan was a man who became willing to change and this willingness brought healing into his life. In his story it is apparent that Namaan suffered from a diseased heart as well as a diseased flesh (leprosy). The pride and anger that dominated his inward man came very close to costing him the answer to prayer he needed.

In order to embrace the future God had for him, Namaan had to humble himself and release these walls from his past. God knew he needed more than just outward physical healing, he needed wholeness. In the end, Namaan's healing also brought a fresh revelation, for he said, *"Indeed, now I know that there is no God in all the earth, except in Israel."*

Are there inward attitudes standing in the way of your healing? As you humble yourself and let go of these walls you will not only open the door to healing, but more importantly, you will open the door to a fresh revelation of God.

CHAPTER FOURTEEN

Turning the Cursing of Our Past into the Blessing of Our Future

Then they came to Elim, where there were twelve wells of water and seventy palm trees; so they camped there by the waters. Exodus 15:27

At the beginning of the book we talked about getting "stuck" in our past. What we really mean by this is that many times people hit difficulties in the present and they decide the outcome of the present situation will be no better than similar situations in the past, so they just "sit down" in their minds, so to speak, and quit.

The truth we need to grasp is that God always has an "Elim" or "answer" just on the horizon, but we will never know that answer if we quit at the "Marahs" in our lives.

The encouraging reality of Marah is that it comes before Elim. Marah is the place where the bitter waters of our life are turned sweet. But again, if we choose not to deal with things at Marah we will never see Elim, the place of blessing.

You may look at certain areas of your life and wonder if there could ever be blessing after everything that has happened and the answer is "yes," if we are willing to trust God and obey the instruction of His voice.

Elim: The Place of Blessing

What actually is this "blessing" we find at Elim? Once again, we will look at the meaning of the name which is *"a grove of oaks or palms, a strong robust tree."* It comes from a root meaning *"to strengthen."* Elim is described as *"... one of the delightful spots found in the desert, where everything grows in such beautiful luxuriance, an exceeding fertile ground."* [26]

I don't think it could be clearer that Elim is the exact opposite of barrenness. It is the place of blessing; the place of the new thing God wants to do in our lives.

> *God always has an "Elim" or "answer" just on the horizon, but we will never know that answer if we quit at the "Marahs" in our life.*

We have seen that Marah - which is located in the Wilderness of Shur or the "place of vision"- is the place where the problem is revealed. The good news, however, is that it is the place where the answer is revealed as well. It is the place where the Devil has tried to curse our life, but it can also be the place where God turns that cursing into blessing.

I have come to love the story of Balaam found in Numbers Chapters 22-24. Balaam was a prophet who was hired by an evil king to curse the Israelites. It gives us a real picture of how the Devil tries to bring cursing into our lives through situations, through people, as well as through our own sins and disobedience. However, the underlying point brought out in all these verses is the Devil cannot curse whom God has blessed, and that is you and me, His children.

Looking back on the account of Balaam and this king, Deuteronomy 23:5 says,

Nevertheless, the Lord your God would not listen to Balaam, but the Lord your God turned the curse into a blessing for you, because the Lord your God loves you.

This is a promise that we can receive and speak over our lives today. I would like you to say this with me now, "The Devil cannot curse whom God has blessed and that is me. I believe God is turning cursing into blessing, He is turning the bitter waters of my life sweet."

Living Life Forward with a New Revelation of God

We have also learned that Marah is the place where another side of God is revealed to us. We find He is our Healer physically, spiritually, and emotionally. Isn't this the most important thing of all? If we will look to God in the bitter waters of life, we will find ourselves coming to know Him in a deeper and more intimate way than ever before. Make no mistake; this always leads us in a path of blessing.

> *When God leads us to Marah and asks us to deal with it, Marah actually becomes a signpost that Elim is next!*

Finally, the last thing that we have discovered is that Marah is the doorway to Elim. Most of the time we become upset when we come to the "Marahs" in our life and we think, "Here it is again! I can't believe this could be happening to me again!" However, when we let our minds travel in this direction, we are looking at it all wrong and this is why: *When God leads us to Marah and asks us to deal with it, Marah actually becomes a sign post that Elim is next*! And not only that, God also wants to take us there. He is leading us into a situation where we can be purified and made ready to go.

Blessing: Temporary or Permanent?

At this point in our study a question could arise: "Do I really need to change? After all, Israel continued to complain and they still went to Elim."

By the grace and mercy of God, Israel did travel on to Elim, and by God's grace and mercy many times you and I will travel there as well. But the thing we must know about Elim is it has what I will call, two "tracks."

The Popular Temporary Track

The first track is the temporary track, also known as "crisis deliverance," and this is exactly what we see demonstrated in the Israelites. Moses interceded on their behalf and God delivered them; however, after a temporary stay at Elim, they had to move on, back out into the wilderness, headed for the next crisis.

Is this not the picture of the lives of many people today? As we said earlier, they want just enough of God to get them through the present crisis, but not enough to keep them out of the next crisis.

When my husband and I minister at the county jail, we encounter people who have been in and out of jail multiple times. Every time they return, they head for the weekly church service provided, but when it comes time to leave again, they don't take Jesus with them; they leave Him in the jail. What they don't understand is the Jesus who ministered to them and helped them through their time in jail is the same Jesus who can keep them out of jail the next time if they will only take Him with them.

What am I saying? *Don't leave Jesus in your present crisis once you get a little relief. If you will take Him with you for good, He can keep you from returning to the same crisis over and over again.*

The Permanent Track to Living Life Forward

Most people are very familiar with Elim's temporary track, however, not as many are acquainted with its second track, which is the permanent track. This is the track we should desire because rather than leading back into the wilderness, it leads directly into the Promised Land. And really there is only one thing that determines which track we will be on: *whether or not we have changed on the inside.*

It is too easy in the Christian life to say the right things and do the right things just enough to get by but not enough to be transformed.

Many of the people we minister to in the jail are there because of addictions. One of the predominant questions we always seem to hear from them is, "Why do I keep going back to it?" Why does any person keep going back to conduct and behaviors not in line with God's Word?

I believe one big answer to this question is just what we are talking about here; there has been no change on the inside of them. As a result, they still see themselves as the person who is addicted, the person who has an anger problem, the person who is always a failure, rather than seeing themselves as God sees them, which is *"more than a conqueror in Christ"* (Romans 8:37).

Early on we mentioned 2 Corinthians 3:18, *"But we all, with unveiled face, beholding as in a mirror the glory of the Lord, are being transformed into the same image from glory to glory, just as by the Spirit of the Lord."*

It is the plan and purpose of God for our lives that we are progressively changed and transformed into the glory of the image of Jesus Christ. This is a transformation that begins first on the inside of us, and then works its way to the outside to affect our circumstances. Philippians 2:12b tells us to *"work out your own salvation with fear and trembling."*

We must read the Bible, pray and communicate with God, attend church, worship God, and obey His Word in such a way that it gets on the inside of us and changes how we view ourselves. *It is too easy in the Christian life to say the right things and do the right things just enough to get by but not enough to be transformed.*

When we look into the mirror of God's Word and we continue looking, it will begin to show us how God sees us in Christ. The deeper we gaze upon the image of Jesus Christ, the more we will be changed into His likeness and nature. This is a must for the victorious Christian life.

Again, looking at Elim, the real key to God turning the bitter waters sweet in our life is the *turn* or the change which happens on the inside of us, where God's "new thing" is finally able to meet up with our new response.

SUMMARY: *Changed into the Image of Jesus Christ*

God is willing to turn our bitter waters sweet. He is ready and willing to turn our cursing into blessing; but we have to also be willing to be changed on the inside into the image of Jesus Christ.

Further Thought

1. I once heard a minister say the book of Job is about what to do when you don't understand. Too many people get hung up on the "why" of their situation. At the end of the book, Job still did not have the answer to "why," but finally understood "what" to do. In response to God's direction, he prayed for the friends who had talked badly of him and when he did, complete restoration came.

Job dealt with his present circumstances by throwing in a "tree" of forgiveness. Because he faced up to and dealt with his "Marah" he was enabled to travel onto "Elim." Job was blessed with twice as much as he had in the beginning.

Have you been stuck in the "why" of your situation? The highway to Elim will be opened up to you when you finally trade your "why" for "what." What is God leading you to do to fully deal with the bondage you have experienced?

2. We have seen in Job's testimony that you can receive healing in your life and be blessed even before you understand the "why" of your situation. We can also see this principle illustrated in the life of Joseph.

In Genesis 41:51-52, Joseph has now been released from prison, he has been exalted to a high government position, and he has been blessed with two sons. He named his firstborn Manasseh, meaning *"For God has made me forget all my toil and all my father's house."* He named his second born Ephraim, meaning, *"For God has caused me to be fruitful in the land of my affliction."* Joseph was able to enjoy great blessing from God because he looked to God to heal the wounds of his past, even before he had any hope of reconciliation with his family in the natural, and even when he still had no answer to the "why" question.

Are you ready to let God do a work in your life and to expect His blessing even though you still don't have all the answers to "why"?

3. You may ask, "Will I ever understand why? Will I ever have an answer?" Truthfully, the greatest answer we can have is when our eyes are finally opened to see how God, in His great mercy, has taken the cursing of our life and turned it into blessing. Once you really get a glimpse of that, everything else fades by comparison.

In Genesis chapter 45, we find a dramatic scene. Overcome by great emotion, Joseph reveals his true identity to his brothers who had wronged him many years before. They are shocked, but Joseph consoles them by explaining the revelation that has come to him: They may have sold him as a slave, but God used that situation to send Joseph ahead of them to preserve life. God went on to position Joseph to be in the right place at the right time in order to keep his family alive in a desperate time of famine. Later in Genesis 50:20 he explained further, *"But as for you, you meant evil against me; but God meant it for good, in order to bring it about as it is this day, to save many people alive."*

The final question I want to ask you is this: "Could it be that God has sent you ahead to not only be blessed, but to preserve the life of others?" When we allow God to do a complete work of healing on the inside of us, it will inevitably affect everyone around us. Your deliverance could and should bring healing into the lives of those God brings into your life.

Conclusion

The Lord builds up Jerusalem; He gathers together the outcasts of Israel. He heals the brokenhearted and binds up their wounds. Psalm 147:2-3

These verses really sum up many of the concepts we have examined in this book. They are referring to a time when the people of Israel had been too busy building their own homes to be bothered with the rebuilding of the temple. However, they finally became obedient to put the building of the temple first. Because they had done this, God was saying He would see to it that the walls of Jerusalem would be built up to protect them. Through this, their broken hearts and wounds would be healed.

What this says to you and me is if we will cease from building our own house – our own walls of protection – and if we will begin to put the building of the temple of God on the inside of us first, allowing God to change us and do a work in our heart, He promises to build supernatural walls of protection around us so He becomes our protector instead of ourselves and as a result, our broken hearts and our wounds will be healed.

Violence shall no longer be heard in your land, neither wasting nor destruction within your borders; but you shall call your walls Salvation, and your gates Praise. Is. 60:18

In that day this song will be sung in the land of Judah: "We have a strong city; God will appoint salvation for walls and bulwarks." Is. 26:1

A PRAYER FOR SALVATION

Heavenly Father, I come to you in the Name of Your Son, Jesus. According to Your Word (Romans 10:9-10), I say with my mouth that I believe Jesus is Your Son. I believe in my heart that You raised Him from the dead. I believe He died in my behalf (Romans 5:6-8). By faith I receive His sacrifice now.

Thank you Jesus for paying the price for my sin (Romans 4:25, 2 Corinthians 5:21). Thank you for making me new (2 Corinthians 5:17) and for giving me a future in You (Jeremiah 29:11-13). From this moment forward I give my life to You. I ask You to lead and guide me and to help me fulfill my purpose in You.

I thank you that I am now saved and I am now Your child. Amen.

If you prayed that prayer today, let me encourage you to do two things immediately: begin reading the Bible everyday and find a good Bible believing church where you can be taught and grow in the things of God.

Rhonda can be contacted by e-mail at
rhondahouston13@aol.com.

Endnotes

1. Zodhiates, Spiros, Th.D., The Complete Word Study Dictionary, New Testament (Chattanooga, TN: AMG Publishers, 1993) p. 482
2. Zodhiates, Spiros, Th.D., The Complete Word Study New Testament (Chattanooga, TN: AMG Publishers, 1991) p. 879
3. Zodhiates, Spiros, Th.D., The Complete Word Study Old Testament (Chattanooga, TN: AMG Publishers, 1994) pp. 160, 2342
4. Harris, R, Laird, and Archer, Gleason L., Jr., and Waltke Bruce K., Theological Wordbook of the Old Testament (Chicago: Moody Press, 1980) 2:723
5. See Ref. 4, 1:51

6. The New Testament from 26 Translations (Grand Rapids, MI: Zondervan Bible Publishers, 1967) p. 1094
7. See Ref. 4, 2:661-662
8. Number in Scripture by E. W. Bullinger, Philologos Religious Online Books, http://philologos.org/_eb-nis/three.htm, (accessed February 11, 2010)
9. See Ref. 3, pp. 164, 2346
10. Andrews, Andy, Mastering The Seven Decisions (Nashville, Dallas, Mexico City, Rio De Janiero, Bejing: Thomas Nelson Publishers, 2008) pp. 4-5
11. See Ref. 4, 2:923
12. Dilday, Russell, Mastering the Old Testament, 1, 2 Kings (Dallas, London, Vancouver, Melbourne: Word Publishing, 1987) p. 271
13. McGrath, Alister and Packer, J.I., eds., The Crossway Classic Commentaries, Psalms Vol. 1, Spurgeon (Wheaton, Illinois: Crossway Books, 1993) p. 193
14. New Spirit Filled Life Bible, NKJV (Nashville, TN: Thomas Nelson Publishers, 2002) pp. 1458-59
15. Hobson, Tim, The Heart of the Matter: Part 2, CD (Montrose, MI: Lamb of God Fellowship, 2010)

16. Gaebelein, Frank E., eds., The Expositor's Bible Commentary (Grand Rapids, MI: Zondervan Publishing House, 1988) 4:177
17. Jones, Alfred, Jones' Dictionary of Old Testament Proper Names (Grand Rapids, MI: Kregel Publications, 1997) p. 340
18. See Ref. 4, 2:661-662
19. See Ref. 3, pp.1480, 87
20. Tenney, Merrill C., eds., The Zondervan Pictorial Encyclopedia of the Bible (Grand Rapids, MI: Zondervan Publishing House, 1976) 5:423-24
21. See Ref. 14, pp. 96-97
22. Lockyer, Herbert, All the Divine Names and Titles in the Bible (Grand Rapids, MI: Zondervan, 1975) p. 24
23. Thompson, J.A., NICOT: The Book of Jeremiah (Grand Rapids, MI: William B. Eerdmans Publishing Company, 1992) pp. 306-7
24. See Ref. 4, 2:687
25. See Ref. 22, p. 5
26. See Ref. 17, p. 108

What I now know —

1) Stop hindering God from bringing something new in His plan for me
2) The Christian life is about making progress
3) We are being changed from Glory to Glory
4) God can "loose" me from my emotional bondage
5) Do not be entangled AGAIN with a yoke of bondage. When I am free — stay free!
6) Freedom — grab hold of it & refuse to let it go
7) Crisis tells me where my Focus, Heart and Trust lie
8) God wants to completely heal me & set me FREE from the control of my past but Satan pressures me to NOT cut my ties.
  * This was the biggest "AHA" for me — & the biggest confirmation of the "ACTION" I needed to do!
9) Accept responsibility of where I am now so I have hope to change my future.

10) This is the time to pursue walking in more of God's power & grace.

11) Allow God to give me a new vision for my future

12) Return & be healed & God will be with me Jer 30:17 Our obedience = blessing

13) Leave my past in Oklahoma — forget what's behind & reach forward to what is ahead

14) Cutting ties w/ the hurts & wounds of my past happens daily & in degrees over time. Daily decide to go forward. Complete deliverance may come little by little in in degrees over time — but it will come! Deut 7:22

15) Stop dragging around the old dead man in my past!

16) Forgive myself

17) Have eyes to see what Jesus did for me & have a willing heart to obey what He shows me to do

18) God is turning the bitter waters of my life sweet

19) God is my healer
   Jehovah Rapha!

LaVergne, TN USA
08 July 2010
188766LV00001B/6/P